THE PICTORIAL HISTORY OF
COLLEGE BASKETBALL

THE PICTORIAL HISTORY OF
COLLEGE BASKETBALL

GALLERY BOOKS
An imprint of W.H. Smith Publishers Inc.
112 Madison Avenue
New York, New York 10016

Contents

Part I
The Early Days

Introduction   7

A Brand New Game   10

Early College Years   16

Part II
The War Years

Headed for the Big Time   24

The Big Men   42

The War Years   48

Part III
Triumphs and Tragedies

The Postwar Basketboom   64

Scandal   78

The Game Comes Back   86

Published by Gallery Books
A Division of W H Smith Publishers Inc.
112 Madison Avenue
New York, New York 10016

Produced by
Brompton Books Corp.
15 Sherwood Place
Greenwich, CT 06830

Copyright © 1989 Brompton Books Corp.

ISBN 0-8317-6902-5

Printed in Portugal

10 9 8 7 6 5 4 3 2 1

PAGES 2-3: Players from Duke and
Notre Dame leap skyward during
1989 action. College basketball on
the whole was also leaping
skyward, as the sport continued to
increase in popularity.

Part IV
Basketball, Supersport

Bruin Dynasty   116

The Ladies Enter   142

Fight for the Final Four   148

Part V
The Contemporary Game

The Eighties   164

Index   191

Introduction

The sport of basketball is a uniquely American game, one that will have its 100th anniversary celebration in the winter of 1991. For it was just a century earlier that James Naismith, responding to a request to devise a new kind of indoor sport activity for the cold-weather months, wrote down the initial guidelines for the new game. The object was to toss a round ball into a goal, which turned out at first to be a rudimentary peach basket attached to the gymnasium wall. It was crude and experimental, but it was in all its essentials basketball.

Though Naismith's game spread quickly, first as a recreational activity and soon thereafter as a collegiate and professional sport, it would still take more than a half century before it permanently established itself alongside baseball and football as a major spectator sport. During that time there would be many kinds of growing pains – flows and ebbs in popularity that resulted in a long period of maturation, as well as the spectre of a widespread scandal involving point-shaving.

Today the sport is played on an international stage. The participants are both men and women at the collegiate and amateur levels in many countries of the world. The very best players can go on to lucrative professional careers, not only in the National Basketball Association, but in pro leagues in Italy, Spain and several other countries.

At the college level basketball may now be entering a new golden age. More and more schools are fielding competitive, entertaining teams that play at an elevated level of skill. Many games are shown on regional and national television, and the NCAA tournament at the end of each season, now a giant 64-team extravaganza, is watched by millions as it winds its way down to the magical Final Four.

Even the women's game has become big time in the 1980s. Universities and colleges are competing for female talent and are offering scholarships. And the ladies no longer play a patty-cake imitation of the real thing: it's a skilled game with first-rate players going full speed at both ends of the court for 40 minutes.

And while the United States is still the perennial favorite in international competition, they don't always win any more. Other nations have been closing the gap. With coaches from America traveling around the world as ambassadors of good will, world basketball has been the beneficiary. Teams from the Soviet Union, Brazil, Spain, Italy, Puerto Rico and Canada have learned how to play the game, and on any given night they are fully capable of playing on the same court with an all-star team of United States collegians.

The top US college players are sought after by the pros and can command huge salaries in the game of play-for-pay. But even as collegians they become heroes not only in their hometowns, but all across the land. Current NBA legends such as Larry Bird, Magic Johnson, Michael Jordan and Akeem Olajuwon were just as popular and well known as collegiate stars.

Yes, the court game has come a long way since the days of Dr. Naismith. And many of those who follow and participate in basketball at any of its many levels feel that the best is yet to come.

It was sometime during his college days at Indiana State that the Larry Bird legend began to grow. One of the greatest collegians ever, Bird continued his great hoop career in the pros.

PART I

The
Early Years

There was a different look to sports as a whole before the turn of the century. This Yale University athletic team of 1890 reflects the style of the period. But they also show the same pride and comaraderie that sports teams have always had.

A Brand New Game

The sport of basketball originated in a rather strange way. Instead of evolving from a series of games which contained elements of several sports, such as was the case with baseball and football, basketball was invented all at once, intentionally, as the direct result of a request.

Dr. Luther H. Gulick was the man who asked for the invention of a new sport. Dr. Gulick was the head of the physical education department of the International Training School of the Young Men's Christian Association in Springfield, Massachusetts, a school that would later become Springfield College. It was the fall of 1891, and Dr. Gulick was trying to remedy what he considered to be an annual winter problem.

He felt that the students at the school just weren't interested in the usual cold weather indoor activities: marching, gymnastics and calisthenics. What the bored students needed, he felt, was some sort of competitive team game that could be played indoors all winter long, some sort of healthy robust activity into which the students could really sink their teeth.

Dr. Gulick then recalled a conversation he had previously had with James Naismith, who was then a 30-year-old physical education instructor at the school. The two men had talked about the possibility of inventing a new game that could be played indoors. With that conversation in mind Dr. Gulick asked Naismith to take over the Phys Ed class and think once again about devising the new game.

As soon as he began working with the students Naismith saw that Dr. Gulick was right, that the students were indeed bored almost to the point of rebellion. The first thing he did was stop the gymnastics and calisthenics and try to concentrate on adapting various traditional outdoor games to indoor play.

Rugby was one such experiment, but it was quickly abandoned because the rough tackling on the gym floor was far too dangerous. Then Naismith tried soccer, but in the small area the players often

kicked each other, as well as breaking a good number of the windows in the gym with strong kicks. The third failure was lacrosse. An aggressive game at best, it became nearly lethal in the constricted space of the gym floor.

Naismith doubtless tried these sports first because he had grown up with them. A native of Almonte, Ontario, Naismith had originally studied to be a minister at McGill University in Montreal. But after three years he had decided he was better suited to physical education, so he had transferred to Springfield and upon graduation had became one of the school's instructors. But it was now all too clear that he would not be able to solve Springfield's problem simply by importing the outdoor games he knew best into Springfield's gym. It had to be an all-new game, and slowly an idea began formulating in his mind.

His new idea involved a large round ball and a game in which the players wouldn't need sticks, racquets or similar kinds of equipment. The next question was what to do with the ball? It was obvious that he couldn't have the players run with it. Indoor football wasn't what he was after. Instead, the ball would have to be thrown. But where, and with what as the object?

After exploring the various possibilities Naismith concluded that the ball would have to be thrown through some kind of goal. And if that goal was somehow placed up high, then the ball would have to be thrown above the heads of the players, eliminating another potential source of injury. And as his ideas began taking shape, Naismith began to sense

LEFT: *James Naismith was a rugged football player shortly before he invented basketball.*

BELOW: *Dr. Luther Gulick.*

OPPOSITE: *The Springfield YMCA.*

that perhaps he *was* on the verge of fulfilling Dr. Gulick's request.

Finally, Naismith sat down and wrote out the first rules for the new game. The next day he went down to the gym and asked the custodian if he could suggest some kind of boxes that could be used as goals. The only thing available was a pair of peach baskets, so Naismith took them in hand and went about the business of nailing them to the end of the balcony that surrounded the gym. He put one at each end, ten feet off the floor and then got ready for his first gym class of the day.

He wasted no time in explaining the new game to the students. He showed them the ball and the baskets and said that a team would score when one of its members could throw the ball through the peach basket. The players were anxious to try the game and at once began to play. Thus mid-December, 1891, witnessed the official birth of the sport of basketball.

When the students went home for Christmas vacation Naismith set about converting his first rough jottings into a full-fledged set of rules for the game. This is the way the students saw the rules posted on the wall when they returned to school in January of 1892.

1. The ball may be thrown in any direction with one or both hands.
2. The ball may be batted in any direction with one or both hands (never with the fist).
3. A player cannot run with the ball. The players must throw it from the spot on which he catches it, allowance to be made for a man who catches the ball when running if he tries to stop.
4. The ball must be held in or between the hands; the arms or body must not be used for holding it.
5. No shouldering, holding, pushing, tripping, or striking in any way the person of any opponent shall be allowed; the first infringement of this rule by any person shall count as a foul, the second shall disqualify

him until the next goal is made, or if there was evident intent to injure the person, for the whole of the game, no substitute allowed.
6. A foul is striking at the ball with the fist, violations of Rules 3, 4, and such as described in Rule 5.
7. If either side makes three consecutive fouls, it shall count as a goal for the opponents (consecutive means without the opponents in the mean time making a foul).
8. A goal shall be made when the ball is thrown or batted from the ground into the basket and stays there, providing those defending the goal do not touch or disturb the goal. If the ball rests on the edges, and an opponent moves the basket, it shall count as a goal.
9. When the ball goes out of bounds, it shall be thrown into the field and played by the person first touching it. He has a right to hold it un-molested for five seconds. In case of a dispute the umpire shall throw it straight into the field. The thrower-in is allowed five seconds; if he holds it longer it shall go to the opponent. If any side persists in delaying the game the umpire shall call a foul on that side.
10. The umpire shall be the judge of the men and shall note the fouls and notify the referee when three consecutive fouls have been made. He shall have the power to disqualify men according to Rule 5.
11. The referee shall be the judge of the ball and shall decide when the ball is in play, in bounds, to which side it belongs, and shall keep the time. He shall decide when a goal has been made, and keep account of the goals, with any other duties that are usually performed by a referee.
12. The time shall be two fifteen minute halves, with five minutes rest between.
13. The side making the most goals in that time shall be declared the winners. In the case of a draw the game may, by agreement of the captains, be continued until another goal is made.

LEFT: *Basketball was firmly established in James Naismith's later years, but the game's inventor still liked to pose with the old ball and peach basket.*

BELOW: *This was one form of basketball played around 1892. The peach basket was suspended on top of the pole and there was no backboard at all.*

OPPOSITE TOP: *An interior photo of the Armory Hill YMCA in Springfield where the first basketball game was played in December, 1891.*

OPPOSITE BOTTOM: *This is Springfield's first basketball team as they looked in December of 1891. James Naismith is wearing the suit and tie.*

While Naismith's original game hardly resembles basketball as it's played today, the essence was there, and some similarities remain intact. The five-second time limit for throwing the ball in bounds is still used today. And he had also decided that the best way to put the ball in play was to toss it in the air between two players, a maneuver that would eventually become the center jump. Naismith also wanted to control the early game by having the referee call fouls. Yet there was no mention of dribbling the basketball. That, and may other things, would come later.

Naismith's original game provided for nine players to a side. This was so that he could get more members of his gym class in action at one time. Yet within a year of the game's invention there was already a provision for five players to a side if the gymnasium was small. In fact, it was the size of the gym that determined the number of players in those very early days. There was a five-, a seven- and nine-player game, and it wasn't until 1897 that five became the official number.

It didn't take Naismith's game long to begin spreading. Had Naismith not protested so vigorously the sport might have been called

"Naismith-ball," as someone had suggested. But when the inventor nixed that one, the next logical choice seemed to be basketball. So basketball it was, and by early 1892 the game was being played in enough places to be written about in the *New York Times*.

The first games were played by Naismith's Springfield team and by other local YMCAs. And in the early days of the game women began playing almost as much as men. This especially pleased Naismith, who had envisioned the game as being for both men and women. In fact, it was while attending a game in March of 1892 between a group of local Springfield women and a team of women teachers that James Naismith met his future wife, Maude Sherman, one of the players in the game.

It also didn't take the game long to begin spreading to the colleges. There is a record of basketball appearing at two women's colleges, Vassar and Smith, as early as 1892, and the men were also beginning to play at about the same time. Naismith himself wrote a description of the archetypal basketball player. "I had in mind the tall, agile, graceful, and expert athlete," was the way he put it, "one who could reach, jump, and act quickly and easily."

During the next few years the early rules began to change. In the original rules a field goal counted just one point. Later, field goals were raised to three points, before dropping back to the present two. A point was originally awarded when the opposing team committed three fouls, but before long that was dropped, and free throws were awarded when fouls were committed. By 1897 the free-throw line was standardized at 15 feet from the hoop.

Other changes also began to appear. The first metal hoops were put in use as early as 1893, and the first backboards came into existence two years later. The sport was certainly not going to remain a peach-basket game forever, especially if it was going to become a major collegiate sport. But it would still be a good number of years before the rules were really standardized.

It also didn't take long for the dribble to come into play, giving the game more flow and avoiding stalemated situations where a pass just couldn't be made. The dribble actually evolved out of another rule that allowed a player to throw the ball in the air and catch it again, in effect a pass to himself. It was as a result of trying to decide what to do when such passes bounced that the dribble was eventually born.

There was another early rule that also had to go. It stipulated that when a ball went out of bounds the first player to touch it would get to throw it back in. This led to some wild dashes after the ball, looking almost like a group of football players chasing a fumble. A new rule, which wasn't really accepted everywhere until about 1913, said that the team last touching the ball *before* it went out of bounds would lose possession. That definitely made more sense and took some more of the early mayhem out of the game.

Scoring in the early days was sometimes incredibly low, with teams often failing to reach ten points. There were no sharpshooters drilling baskets from all over the court. One YMCA tournament, for example, held in 1896 to determine the "Champion of America," resulted in the

East District "Y" of Brooklyn defeating Brooklyn Central by the unlikely score of 4-0.

But the game was growing and would continue to grow. It would spread from the YMCAs to the colleges, and then to the high schools. Teams would also begin playing professionally before long, barnstorming around their local areas looking for other games and whatever guarantees they might be able to get. Colleges weren't yet offering scholarships or seeking the best players, but, like all other college activities, the sport was rapidly becoming highly competitive.

The game's inventor didn't stay at Springfield long, but he didn't abandon his new sport when he left. In 1895 Naismith went to a YMCA

ABOVE LEFT: *Dr. Naismith always wanted women to be part of the hoop game. His wife, Maude, agreed, having played the game herself as a young woman.*

ABOVE RIGHT: *As a professor at Kansas University, Dr. Naismith continued to teach the game to women as well as men.*

RIGHT: *Senda Berenson (in long dress) gets set to start play in the first public women's game at Smith College in 1893.*

in Colorado, where he also returned to school and became a medical doctor in 1898. But even with his degree he decided to remain in physical education, his first love.

Eventually he was appointed head of the Phys Ed department of the University of Kansas in 1898. And wherever James Naismith went basketball was sure to follow. He coached the university's team for nine seasons, and upon his retirement from coaching he remained a faculty member at Kansas until his retirement from teaching in 1937.

Dr. James Naismith died in 1939 at the age of 78. At the time of his death the sport he has invented was already firmly entrenched all over the United States, at both the high school and college levels. And while

the professional game was still not on a par with football and baseball, at least Dr. Naismith knew that there were men making money by playing the game he had invented and loved.

Today, of course, the sport is played on the international level. But it's also played in backyards, on playgrounds, in alleys, anyplace where kids can put up a hoop. And in the colleges the game has grown to epic proportions. Almost every school, large and small, has men's and women's teams competing on an intercollegiate level, and the NCAA tournament at the end of each season has become one of the most popular and colorful events in all sport.

James Naismith would have loved that.

ABOVE: *Dr. Naismith (center) and the 1923 Kansas U. team. To Naismith's left is "Phog" Allen, who would take over the Jayhawks and become a legendary coach in his own right.*

LEFT: *Another picture from basketball's early days. The hoop is hooked to the wall with the bottom sewn closed. Note the lack of markings on the court.*

Early College Years

The YMCAs were the first vehicles used to spread the word about the new sport. At the turn of the century almost every town had its own "Y", and most people who enjoyed athletics used the facilities sooner or later. That included many college students, as well as their coaches, so it wasn't long before they learned about this new game that had come out of Springfield. In short order the game was being introduced to the campuses themselves, first at the intramural level, then as a form of intercollegiate competition.

One of the early advocates of intercollegiate basketball was Amos Alonzo Stagg, who is more widely remembered for his many contribu-

tions to college football. Stagg had been in Springfield when Dr. Naismith had started the sport, and he began playing it almost immediately at the "Y." Then, in the autumn of 1892, Stagg became the first athletic director at the University of Chicago, and he brought the new game with him.

Before long Stagg had many of his students playing the game among themselves, and by 1894 he had started a varsity team at the school. The problem was that no other schools were playing yet, so he had to schedule games against the other local "Y" clubs in the area. But by 1896 Chicago played its first intercollegiate game, against Iowa.

LEFT: *Famous football coach Amos Alonzo Stagg as he appeared in 1899. Stagg was also an early advocate of basketball.*

OPPOSITE TOP: *The Geneva College basketball team of 1891 had a look all its own. But the little school from Beaver Falls, Pennsylvania, was the first to make basketball a college sport.*

OPPOSITE BOTTOM: *Pioneer basketball coach Raymond P. Kaighn, another Naismith disciple.*

And there were others. Iowa, as mentioned, began playing in 1893; Ohio State started a year later; Temple, in Philadelphia, began about the same time; and Yale introduced basketball to the Ivy League the year after that. Other Naismith disciples were already spreading the game elsewhere at the college level.

Many contend that the very first intercollegiate program began at Geneva College in Beaver Falls, Pennsylvania, in February of 1892. The man who brought the game to Geneva was Charles O. Bemies of Boston, also a Springfield alumnus. And the man who started basketball so early at Iowa was Dr. Henry F. Kallenberg, who was a friend of both Naismith and Stagg.

Another former Naismith colleague, Ray Kaighn, organized a team at Hamline University in St. Paul, Minnesota, in 1893. Their first game was against the Minneapolis "Y" and was played in the basement of the Science Building at the school, which had a nine-foot ceiling. Hamline lost that one, 13-12, in a game of basement basketball that must have been a sight to behold.

Hamline was also involved in what was the first officially recorded game between two colleges. In February, 1895, Hamline was beaten by the Minnesota State School of Agriculture by a score of 9-3. A month later, Haverford College of Pennsylvania defeated Temple by a 6-4 score. A man named Charles M. Williams had started the sport at Temple, and he had also been a student of Naismith's at Springfield.

The Naismith connection continued to help spread the sport. Because Stagg and Kallenberg were friends, they decided to have a home-and-home series between Chicago and Iowa in 1896. Chicago won both games by scores of 15-12 and 34-18. The two games marked the first intercollegiate contests played with five men to a side, a practice that would soon become universal. When Yale joined the basketball ranks in 1895 the players wore football pants and socks. The University of Pennsylvania began playing two years later, in 1897, and it

began to look more and more as if the new sport was destined to become a permanent part of college athletics.

The early growth of the sport was hindered somewhat by a lack both of facilities and standardization of the rules. One night a team might play in a real gymnasium, but the next night they could be in a basement with nine-foot ceilings and pillars right out on the court. One opponent might insist on the five-men-to-a-side game, while the next might refuse to play unless there were seven on a side. At one point the University of Pennsylvania actually dropped the sport because of a lack of adequate facilities. After a four-year absence, between 1898 and 1902, Penn returned. Yale, in the meantime, had gone on a tour of the Midwest and had played in the first intersectional collegiate games. The game spread from Yale to archrival Harvard when a Yale grad named John Kirkland Clark enrolled in Harvard Law School and promptly organized a club team. Within a year the Crimson had a varsity ballclub, with Clark serving as both coach and captain.

With more and more schools playing the game, the next logical step seemed to be leagues. Sure enough, in 1901 an Eastern League was formed, with Yale winning the first title over the likes of Princeton, Columbia, Cornell and Harvard. It was the forerunner of today's Ivy League. The same year, a number of schools to the north – Amherst, Dartmouth, Holy Cross, Williams and Trinity – formed the New England League.

A year later, in 1902, basketball came to the United States Military Academy at West Point. The cadet who started the sport was Joseph Stillwell, who would become famous as General "Vinegar Joe" Stillwell during World War II. And by 1905 a number of midwestern schools – Indiana, Chicago, Purdue, Wisconsin, Minnesota and Illinois – joined the new Western Conference, the forerunner of the Big Ten.

OPPOSITE TOP: *A turn-of-the-century University of Pennsylvania team.*

OPPOSITE BOTTOM: *Penn Athletic Director Ralph Morgan organized college coaches into a group that eventually became the National Collegiate Athletic Association (NCAA).*

ABOVE: *Bloomer-clad girls playing an indoor game in 1900.*

LEFT: *An outdoor women's game played at Arkansas State Teachers College, also about 1900.*

Minnesota was the early superpower of the area. The Gophers won 34 straight games between 1902 and 1904, and in the first year of the new Western Conference they became its champion. The rapid growth of the sport and the schools' rush to form teams also caused some interesting mismatches. For example, in 1903 Bucknell University defeated the Philadelphia College of Pharmacy by the incredible score of 159-5. A player named John Anderson from Bucknell scored 80 points in the romp. Who said their were no Larry Birds or Michael Jordans back then?

At Illinois the introduction of basketball took an even more unusual turn: it was the ladies who began playing the game first. Their gym was the loft of the Natural History Building, and the men began to sneak up there to watch the games. Often the couples ended up dancing instead of playing basketball. When the university president learned what was happening he promptly banned the sport. It came back in 1903, but once again for women only. It wasn't until the Western Conference was formed two years later that a men's team was finally started.

Even in these early days teams were interested in testing their mettle against ballclubs from other parts of the country. In 1904 there was a national outdoor tournament held in St. Louis, and little Hiram College emerged the winner. A year later Columbia was putting the finishing touches on 26-game winning streak. As soon as that season ended the Lions arranged games against Minnesota and Wisconsin. When the Lions won both of these they promptly declared themselves national champions.

Chicago was the big power in the Midwest between 1906 and 1910, winning the Western Conference championship four of the five years. And in 1908, when the club defeated Penn in a home-and-home series, *they* promptly claimed the national title. So even though a nationwide tournament was still some 30 years away, the thought of being the national champion, the best, was already an intriguing one to many schools as they looked for ways to proclaim prowess.

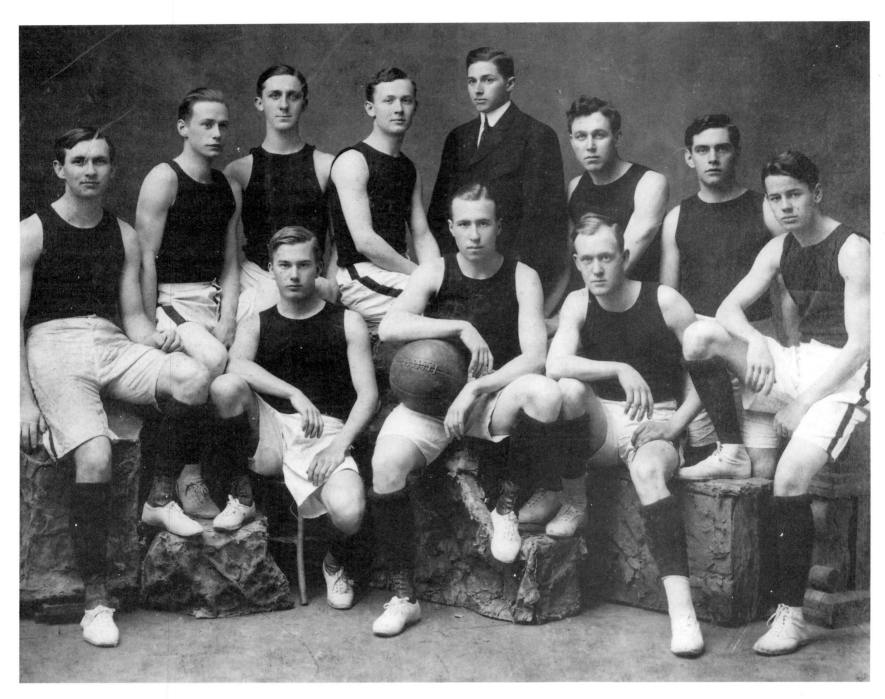

As with other sports in their infancy, the rapid growth of the court game didn't always go smoothly. For one thing, there was no one governing body for the college game, and thus the different leagues and sections of the country didn't always have standardized rules. Discipline was also sometimes lacking, and there was increasingly rough play during the first decade of the twentieth century. In fact, to some basketball was starting to look more like indoor football.

In the very early years some control continued to be exercised over the game by YMCA officials. But this was really a holdover from the game's infancy, and as basketball continued to grow among the colleges any leftover YMCA control fell away. Dr. Luther Gulick was himself one who wanted to see the control given to the Amateur Athletic Union (AAU), but many colleges refused to accept AAU authority, and the result was a perpetuation of anarchy.

AAU authority was most gravely challenged during the 1904-05 season, when the organization decided to prevent Yale from playing an allegedly unregistered team. But university officials turned a deaf ear and continued their schedule. There was an upcoming game against Penn, and the AAU decided to take another approach. This time they told the Penn team that if it took the floor against Yale it would also court suspension.

But Penn coach Ralph Morgan was outraged because he looked on this as something akin to blackmail. Not only did he refuse to cancel the game, he invited athletic directors and coaches from more than 350 colleges to come to Philadelphia for a meeting in April, 1905. The purpose, he told them, was to find a way for the colleges to get control of their own game.

When representatives of only 15 schools arrived in Philly for the meeting it seemed that the whole thing might collapse. But Morgan was resolute. Instead of waiting for more representation or reschedul-

ABOVE: Compared to other early photos, this Princeton team of 1905 has a much more modern look. Yet the game they played was very different from today's. Shooting skills weren't good, there was a center jump after each score and there were no seven-foot giants operating around the hoop.

OPPOSITE TOP: Yale's team of 1901 had a definitely relaxed and casual look. But the Ivy League back then was already very competitive in the new sport.

OPPOSITE BOTTOM: President Theodore Roosevelt opposed the increasing roughness of basketball.

ing the meeting, he formed a committee of seven men and asked them to formulate a set of standardized college rules to be presented before a second meeting, which would be scheduled that summer.

Meeting in New York City in July, 1905, were representatives from Yale, Columbia, Princeton and Pennsylvania. Sitting through a long work session, these determined men accomplished two important things. First, they wrote out the first set of collegiate basketball rules, and, second, they outlined the structure of another organizational meeting that would result in the formation of the Intercollegiate Athletic Association. Although it didn't happen overnight, the Intercollegiate Athletic Association would eventually become the National Collegiate Athletic Association (NCAA), which is still the governing body for college sports today.

That was a good beginning, but another problem that still had to be faced was the rising tide of criticism of the sport resulting from the increasingly rough style of play at many colleges. This came to a head in 1909, the same year that President Theodore Roosevelt voiced serious concern about the growing number of serious injuries in college football. There were some who felt basketball was headed down

the same road, and the young Intercollegiate Athletic Association had its first real battle.

In the spring of 1909 officials at Harvard announced that basketball was being discontinued because the sport was losing popularity at the school. But according to one member of the committee that made the decision at Harvard the real reason was that "The games more closely resembled free fights than friendly athletic contests between amateur teams." But was this in fact the reason? Some thought that it was much more elementary than that. Harvard had a losing program which they couldn't seem to turn around. So instead of changing coaches or looking for better players, they decided to abolish the sport, a decision that would not be reversed for some ten years.

Whatever the reasons for Harvard's defection, no larger consequences in the form of public outcry or legislation ensued. The game was basically left alone to police itself. Several rule changes were made with the intention of getting some of the hooliganism out of the game. In 1908 there was a rule that would disqualify a player after he had committed five personal fouls in a game. And in 1910 a second official was added to games, another step to cut down on rough play.

By 1915 the AAU finally agreed to meet with the YMCAs and the International Athletic Association to standardize the rules for amateur play everywhere. That also went a long way to stabilize and legitimize the game. In a sense, that meeting really marked the end of an era. The sport of basketball had survived its early years and had grown and developed at the college level to the point where it was well organized, accepted, and continuing to grow. In effect, the game had firmly established itself at the college level. Now it was time for those who sensed the future to begin aiming for the heights, for a time when college basketball would not just be accepted but would rank among the most popular sports in the land.

PART II

The War Years

One of the first dominant big men the game has known, DePaul's George Mikan (with glasses), led college basketball's growth in the 1949s. Here Mikan clogs the middle in a 1945 game against Marquette.

Headed for the Big Time

The proliferation of outstanding teams during the period between 1910 and 1920 pointed up still another need. To continue its rapid growth at the college level basketball needed better stages on which to showcase its product. There were some schools that still played the game outdoors, while others were forced to perform in old, outdated gymnasiums built long before the sport was invented. New field houses, stadiums and arenas would soon become a nationwide priority.

The need was underscored even more by the publicity some of the great early teams were receiving. It is now almost forgotten, for instance, that the University of Texas had one of basketball's great early teams. The Longhorns have always been known for their prowess on the gridiron, but from 1913 to 1917 the eyes of Texas were on the Longhorn basketball team. And they deserved it.

Texas was one of the schools which still played the game outdoors, and like many teams that played under the open sky, losses could easily be blamed on the weather. (Funny how it always affected only the losing team.) At any rate, at the tail end of the 1912-1913 season the Longhorns began to win, taking their final three games of that campaign. The next year they were perfect, at 11-0. The following season the club won all 14 of its games, and in 1915-16 they had a 12-0 mark.

By that time all of Texas was looking with pride on its basketball team. And when the club won its first four games the following season it had run its winning streak to an amazing 44 games, the greatest

streak in college ball to that time. Even when the club was finally beaten by Rice, 24-18, the Longhorns were still the toast of Texas.

Interestingly, the ballclub had manufactured its great winning streak under four different coaches. Perhaps the best of the bunch was R.B. Henderson, a Longhorn alumnus who coached the club for just one season, the 12-0 campaign of 1915-16. Stressing a wide-open offensive game, Henderson watched as his ballclub ran up 560 points to just 185 for the opposition. And in their first game of the season that year they outscored San Marcos Baptist by an unreal 102-1.

The star players of those Texas teams are now a distant memory except for perhaps a few diehard fans who have undertaken to read about the school's hoop history. The team's leading scorer was Clyde Littlefield, while Gus "Pig" Dittmar was considered the top defensive player. Pete Edmond was a third outstanding player on those Texas teams of long ago.

Perhaps the most important byproduct of that incredible win streak was the university's decision to build a new indoor gymnasium. Which was begun after the 1916 season. Unfortunately, by the time it was finished most of the players who had put Texas basketball on the map had been graduated, and the team was on the downslide. But at least the school now had a fieldhouse, and their decision to invest in the future of basketball undoubtedly served as a model to others.

Great as they were, the Texas teams weren't the only powerful and

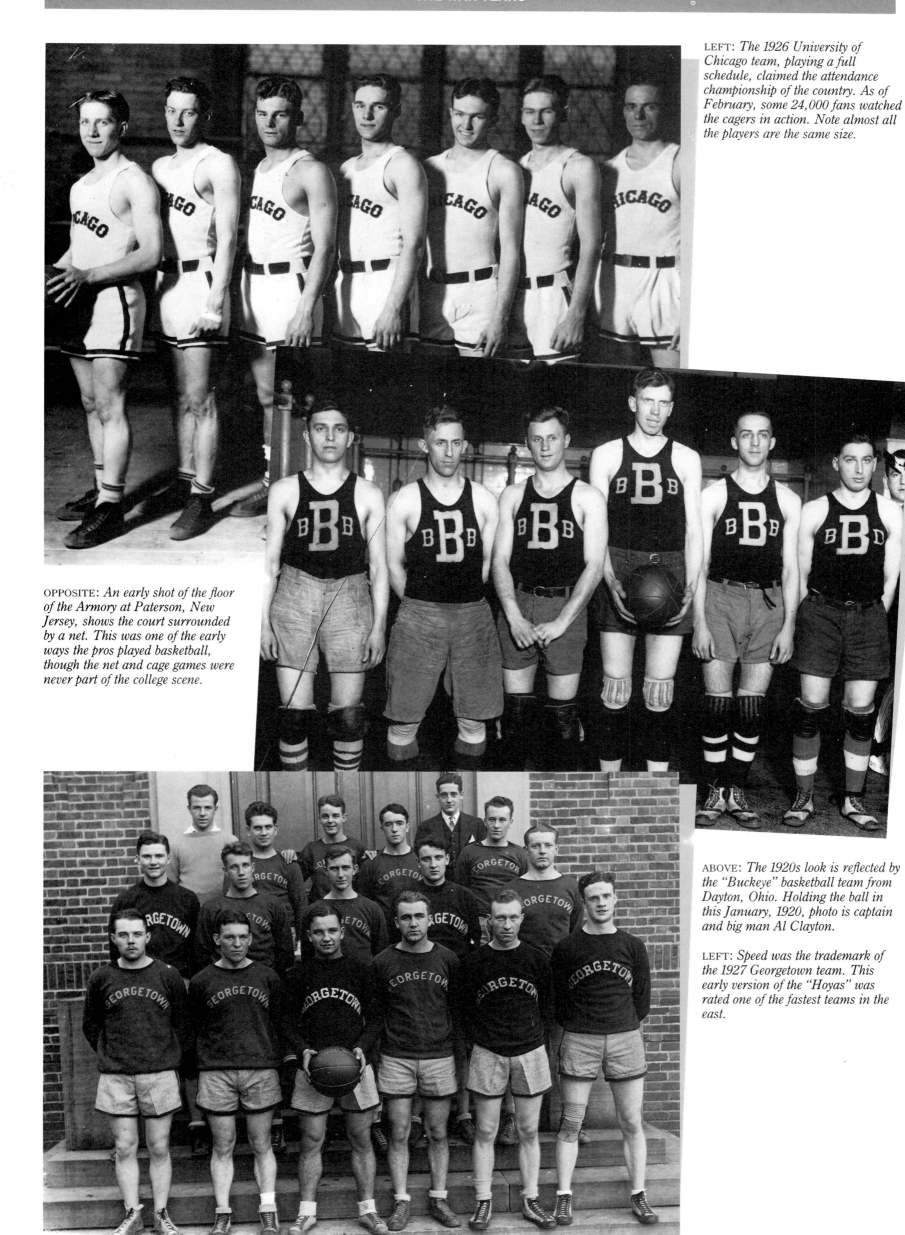

LEFT: *The 1926 University of Chicago team, playing a full schedule, claimed the attendance championship of the country. As of February, some 24,000 fans watched the cagers in action. Note almost all the players are the same size.*

OPPOSITE: *An early shot of the floor of the Armory at Paterson, New Jersey, shows the court surrounded by a net. This was one of the early ways the pros played basketball, though the net and cage games were never part of the college scene.*

ABOVE: *The 1920s look is reflected by the "Buckeye" basketball team from Dayton, Ohio. Holding the ball in this January, 1920, photo is captain and big man Al Clayton.*

LEFT: *Speed was the trademark of the 1927 Georgetown team. This early version of the "Hoyas" was rated one of the fastest teams in the east.*

25

OPPOSITE: *Harlow Rothert, captain of the Stanford teams of 1928-30.*

ABOVE: *Navy starters in 1927.*

RIGHT: *Holding the outsize trophy is Joey Schaaf, of the University of Pennsylvania, in 1929.*

unbeaten ballclubs of that era. Wisconsin had a perfect season in 1914, followed by Illinois and Virginia the next year. Oregon State turned the trick in 1918, Navy in 1919 and Texas A & M in 1920. Even a school such as Montana State was playing outstanding basketball back then. The Bobcats started building a strong team in the late teens, and the momentum carried it right into the 1920s. The club was 19-1 as early as 1917 and compiled a 13-0 mark three years later. Ott Romney was the most successful coach there, compiling an impressive 144-31 mark between 1923 and 1928.

Even Army began getting basketball fever. The United States Military Academy team was being beaten regularly by their Naval counterparts, so in 1923 they hired Coach Harry Fisher away from Columbia, and Fisher proceeded to lead the Cadets to a perfect 17-0 season in his first year. From there he ran the winning streak to 31 before his club finally lost a ballgame.

North Carolina and Texas were again unbeaten in 1924, each compiling 23-0 records, and by now the season was beginning to stretch out with additional games. But while these various teams were taking turns putting together outstanding seasons there were some other problems that had to be dealt with as the sport continued to grow. For one thing, most teams still continued to play within their own sections of the country. If, for example, a Texas and a Montana State were both unbeaten there was very little chance of them meeting to see which played the better brand of basketball. Yet coaches, players and fans all wanted to see more inter-sectional play. A combination of curiosity and pride was the motivation, as well as a simple case of finding out who was the best.

Then there were the rules. Some of the holdover regulations from the early days were obviously hindering the development of a faster and smoother game. Many games were deteriorating into nothing more than a succession of free throws, with the players walking slowly up and down the court: it seemed as if the refs' whistles never stopped. At that time foul shots were awarded for infractions such as traveling and double dribbling. Finally, in 1923, these things were designated as violations, with the only penalty being the loss of the ball. A quick out-of-bounds play was a lot more desirable than trudging down to the other end for a free throw.

Another rule that hung on until the late 1930s was the center jump after each basket. This one had been on the books since the beginning, but it really slowed play. Whenever a hoop was scored everyone marched back to center court and lined up for a jump ball. That eliminated both a smooth transition and the possibility of the fastbreak, and also kept the scores down. How much the persistence of this rule hindered the growth of basketball's popularity is moot, but it didn't help.

While there were outstanding teams from all sections of the country, the New York area had remained a competitive hotbed of the court game almost from the beginning. And it was in New York in March, 1920, that an event took place that proved once and for all that basketball was a sport of enormous potential both in fan appeal and in financial terms. It started with an already intense rivalry that had the entire city hopping.

The two schools involved were New York University and City College of New York. They would play each other every year with games intense and hard-fought, and the rivalry continued to grow and grow. By 1920 both teams were in the midst of outstanding seasons as their annual meeting approached. NYU had an 11-1 mark, and CCNY would enter the game with a 13-2 record. At that time NYU didn't even have its own gym and was always searching for places to play. But basketball courts were sometimes hard to find, and the team actually played a few of its games on a barge on the Hudson River.

Because of the lack of facilities, it was finally decided to put the 1920 meeting between the two schools into the 168th Street Regiment Armory. Word of the impending game spread quickly, and when the two teams finally squared off there were nearly 10,000 rabid basketball fans crowded into the Armory. It was one of the largest crowds ever to witness a basketball game to that time, and the fans got their money's worth as NYU turned on the afterburners and reaped a big 39-21 victory.

The win was no fluke. Led by their star player, Howard Cann, the Violets went on to win the AAU title in Atlanta a few weeks later, topping another area team, Rutgers, for the title. But basketball officials continued to buzz about the CCNY game and the huge crowd that had been turned on by the spectacle. They knew the sport was beginning to acquire great drawing power and that sooner or later something would have to be done about it. Barges on the Hudson only served to downgrade the game, but it was still up to the individual universities to build their own fieldhouses and arenas.

Then, in the late 1920s, another New York City team began capturing headlines with a style of play that would eventually lead to several more major rule changes. The school was St. John's University, and between 1929 and 1931 its basketball team was so good that its players earned the collective nickname "The Wonder Five."

OPPOSITE BOTTOM: *Eldon Mason was a hard-nosed guard for the University of Minnesota.*

OPPOSITE TOP: *A 1921 YMCA demonstration shows a flagrant foul.*

ABOVE: *After winning the AAU trophy in March of 1920, the NYU team declared itself national champion and was greeted by a wildly enthusiastic university.*

LEFT: *This was part of the huge welcome given the NYU team after its AAU title game win over Rutgers in 1920.*

During the 1931 season the Wonder Five took part in a basketball spectacular that helped to change the face of the game in future years. It happened on January 21, 1931, just a little over a year after the stock market crash of 1929 and the beginning of the Great Depression in the United States. New York City, like so many other areas of the country, was filled with unemployed people who simply could not find work. The then Mayor of New York, James J. Walker, announced that he was sponsoring a basketball tripleheader at Madison Square Garden. The gate from the games would benefit the City's unemployed.

It was a unique format, never before attempted, and because there were three games the time for each half was dropped from 20 to 15 minutes. The extravaganza attracted more than 16,000 basketball fans to the huge arena, and they saw some fine basketball under the rules of the day. In the opener Columbia defeated Fordham by a 21-18 score. This was followed by Manhattan's 16-14 victory over NYU. Then the Wonder Five took the court and came away with a 17-9 triumph over CCNY. The St. John's team concentrated on defense that night and put a smothering blanket over the CCNY attack. City College scored the first basket of the night and then did not score another point from the floor until the final minute of the game.

The tripleheader was a huge success financially. The city collected some $20,000 for the needy and unemployed, but in watching three consecutive low-scoring, close games, many of the fans in attendance realized that something was still wrong with the sport they had grown to love.

For one thing, the pace of the games was slow. There was very little sustained action because of the center jump and the lack of a backcourt rule. In fact, when the Wonder Five went into their slowdown game against CCNY, many fans actually began to boo. They obviously wanted more action, more shooting and higher scores.

The lords of the game knew that something had to be done. So before the 1932 season began a center line was finally painted across the middle of college basketball courts, and the 10-second rule became a reality. Now the offensive team had only ten seconds to bring the ball over that mid-court line and once over, could not bring it back again. And there was another change just over the horizon. That was the

three-second rule, which went into effect in 1935. That rule allowed offensive players in the foul lane for just three seconds. Then they had to get out again or be called for a violation. No longer could an offensive player stand under the basket and block out defenders while waiting for an easy chippie. That rule, too, put more movement and more strategy into the game.

Just a quick postscript on the Wonder Five. The team's starters were all declared ineligible after the 1931 season when it was learned that they had played a few unauthorized games against professionals. So what did the players do? The obvious thing. They turned professional as a group, becoming first the Brooklyn Jewels and later the New York Jewels. And as pros, the former St. John's Wonder Five were still a highly skilled and successful basketball team, competing at the same high level they had shown in college.

All these changes were building blocks for the future. And besides the needed revision in rules, there were already a number of coaches and other people connected with the game who were also looking to the future and were changing the faces of their teams. One such coach was Frank Keaney, who led the Rhode Island State clubs of the early

1930s. Keaney didn't like the slowdown basketball played by the Wonder Five and many other teams. His ballclubs, he said, would do it his way. And his way meant a running game, including a fast-breaking offense, long passes and as many shots as the team could get. Keaney's Rhode Island State teams were the first of what were then called "point a minute" ballclubs, using an offense that can still be found today, an offense known as "run-and-gun" in modern terms. Coaches like Frank Keaney showed there was more than one way to play the game, and the fans loved it. Why see the same thing at every game? Racehorse basketball might not always be foolproof, but it was fun. And with coaches willing to try new things, the game could only go forward as the years passed.

The famous 1931 tripleheader at the Garden had been promoted by Dan Daniel, then a sportswriter with the *New York World Telegram.* Daniel had needed an assistant to organize such a mammoth event, and he had picked one of the newspaper's young writers who was familiar with the college basketball beat. His name was Ned Irish, and he had had to spend more than enough of his time in crowded gymnasiums and other places where college ball sometimes was played.

as CCNY, St. John's and NYU were all considered major powers already, and in the mid-1930s they would have company from another area school, and a rather unlikely one at that. The team from Long Island University, under Coach Clair Bee suddenly began to act as though they were as good as anyone. And they were.

Bee was an innovator, a man not afraid to try new things and one who knew how to get the most out of his available talent. And when that talent was considerable, as it was in the mid-30s, Bee quickly built himself a powerhouse. In 1934 the whippet-thin coach directed his Blackbirds to a 26-1 record. But because LIU played its home games in a tiny, out-of-the-way gym at the Brooklyn College of Pharmacy, not too many people really thought of them as a basketball power.

The 1935-36 season saw the Blackbirds en route to an unbeaten season. The club had some outstanding personnel. All-America Julie Bender was the quarterback, controlling the ball from his guard spot. Another guard, Leo Merson, had a deadly accurate two-hand set shot. Forwards Ken Kramer and Marius Russo were both outstanding. (If Russo's name sounds familiar the answer is, yes, he *was* the same Marius Russo who later pitched in the majors with the New York Yankees.) But the player around whom everything revolved was center Art Hillhouse, who was 6ft 6in and knew how to use his height to the best advantage.

By the middle of the 1936-37 season it was impossible to ignore LIU any longer. Clair Bee's team had a 43-game winning steak over three seasons and was now acknowledged as one of the best teams in the country. And now, at last, they were about to come into Madison Square Garden for a December 30, 1936, clash against Stanford University. The game held great interest because not only was it a rare meeting between teams from the East and West Coasts, but it was also a matchup of two powerhouse ballclubs with contrasting styles. The game would, in fact, be one of the classic confrontations in college basketball history.

Stanford had a star player who was not only able to dominate a game, but who would also leave his mark on the sport for all the years to come. His name was Angelo "Hank" Luisetti, and he was one of the first players to use a one-hand shot. Up to that time there had been two basic shots in basketball. One was the driving layup and the other the

OPPOSITE: *More Garden action featuring St. John's and CCNY in early 1936. The New York teams always had a heated rivalry, making the Garden a noisy place indeed. Battling underneath for the rebound is CCNY star Bernie Fliegal (12).*

ABOVE: *LIU's Julie Bender.*

BELOW: *Coach Clair Bee had another great LIU team in 1938-39. L. to R. Dan Kaplowitz, George Newman, Art Hillhouse, Irv Torgoff, John Bromberg.*

LEFT: *This is the great 1936 Stanford team that came east to show its stuff. L. to R., Arthur Stoefen, Hank Luisetti, Howard Turner, Dinty Moore and Jack Caldewood.*

BELOW: *Hank Luisetti, one of the first one-handed shooters, was perhaps the greatest scorer of his time.*

OPPOSITE: *Despite his huge college success, Hank Luisetti never played professional ball.*

two-handed set shot, which was taken with both feet set and on the ground. But Hank Luisetti had grown up with a different type of game. He was raised in San Francisco and first learned his unique way of shooting from coach Tommy DeNike at Galileo High School. DeNike had shown a number of his players the one-hand shot, but he said he knew from the first that Luisetti was the one who would be able to make something of it.

"A number of my players would use the shot in practice," the coach once said, "but they would only use it in a game once in a while. Hank was different. He wasn't afraid to take the shot in a game. And while the others used it, nobody took it quite like Hank."

By 1936 Hank Luisetti was a 6ft 2½ in All-American who could do a lot more on a basketball court besides shoot the one-hander. He played a total team game, was a tough defensive player and could even go behind the back with the dribble on occasion. So while the one-hand shot was the publicity maker, Luisetti could beat you in a lot of different ways.

Up to that time, many college coaches simply would not allow one-handed shooting. When Luisetti first arrived at Stanford he had to ask his coach, John Bunn, for permission to continue shooting one-handed. If Bunn had any doubts they all but disappeared when he saw the speed with which Luisetti got the shot off. And on top of that, the shot was accurate. Not only could Luisetti shoot flat-footed, he could also take the one-hander off the dribble, making it look similar to a running jump shot. Bunn was too smart a coach to tamper with something like that, and he told Luisetti to keep doing it his way.

There were more than 18,000 cheering fans on hand to witness the clash between Stanford and LIU. And it didn't take Hank Luisetti long to show everyone that he wasn't some West Coast wonder. He was the real thing, the dominant player at both ends of the court. He turned the crowd on with his running one-handers, but he also made an impact at the other end, playing great defense and scrubbing the boards for rebounds.

With Luisetti cooking on both burners and his Stanford teammates raising their own games to a higher level, the Indians dominated from the opening tap. LIU was never in it, and Stanford defeated the Blackbirds 45-31. Luisetti led the way, with 15 points, and received a tumultuous standing ovation from the big crowd. Then, as now, New York fans appreciated an outstanding basketball performer. And with so much attention being given Luisetti and his Stanford teammates, not many people had time to remember that the LIU 43-game win streak,

one of the longest ever to that time, had come to an end.

Hank Luisetti was no fluke. He would end his four-year Stanford career with a new national scoring record of 1596 points. And toward the end of his career Luisetti benefitted from the abolition of perhaps the last of basketball's antiquated rules from the early days, for up until 1937 there was still a center jump after each and every basket. Some traditionalists felt that without the center jump, the pace of the game would actually be too fast, that players couldn't handle it without the brief rest that stopping for a center jump gave them. This, of course, proved to be completely untrue after the rule was changed, but at the time perhaps a more compelling argument for change was that because the clock continued to run during the pause for the center jump there were some nine to 12 minutes of potential playing time being lost in each game. So before the start of the 1937-38 season, the old rule finally bit the dust. It had gone the way of the peach basket, the nine-men-to-a-side game, fouls shots for traveling and double dribbles and many other rules from basketball's earliest days.

The effects of the change were seen almost immediately. With no center jump after each hoop offenses opened up, and the game was noticeably faster. In the first doubleheader of the year, St. John's and Illinois set a Madison Square Garden scoring record in a game won by the Illini 60-45. And on January 1, 1938, Hank Luisetti got into the act when he electrified the basketball world by scoring 50 points in a game against Duquesne. It was the abolition of the center jump that made it possible.

Even though he was the darling of the basketball world, Hank Luisetti never played as a professional. Instead, he chose a career in business and played briefly in an AAU league. To be sure, pro ball didn't offer a very secure future in those days, so Hank Luisetti probably made the right choice. Nevertheless, the man who pioneered the one-hand shot remains a basketball legend, an innovator who helped shape the future of his sport.

The example of Hank Luisetti and the abolition of the center tap opened up all kinds of possibilities. And it didn't take long for a creative thinker like Ned Irish to put another new idea in motion. Irish and a few others began making plans for a big post-season tournament to be held

at Madison Square Garden, which had become college basketball's showcase arena. Irish and his colleagues crystallized their plans during the winter of 1938. The tournament would be sponsored by the Metropolitan Basketball Writers Association and would be called the National Invitation Tournament. For the first event, the organizers wanted an east-west flavor, and the six teams invited were NYU, Colorado, LIU, Oklahoma A&M, Temple and Bradley. Temple, from Philadelphia, came in with the best record, a 23-2 regular-season mark. So the Owls were the favorites as the first NIT began.

The first game was a beauty. NYU and arch-rival LIU battled for 40 minutes, the Violets coming out on top by a 39-37 count. Game two saw Temple dominate Bradley and come away with a 53-40 victory. In the semifinals Colorado just got by NYU, 48-47, while Temple took Oklahoma A&M 54-44. Now it would be Temple against Colorado in the first-ever NIT final.

As an interesting sidenote, one of the Colorado stars was Byron "Whizzer" White, who would become a football All-American for the Buffalos and much later a justice on the United States Supreme Court.

But it took more than the exceptional White to help Colorado in the finals. Playing before a packed house of cheering fans, Temple easily outscored the Buffalos 60-36, to take the first NIT championship. In the minds of many the Owls were thus the national champions.

Not only was the NIT a rousing success, it quickly led to more post-season action. Seeing just how well a nationwide tournament could work, the National Collegiate Athletic Association decided to sponsor a tournament of its own the following season. For a number of years, both tourneys would compete on equal footing, but eventually the NCAA event would become the showcase for the national championship, one of the premier events in American sport. Yet at the end of the 1930s there were two, and for the first time north could meet south and east could meet west on neutral courts, and basketball fans could not only follow their favorite teams, but could also compare the styles of basketball played nationwide and the great players who were now coming out of every section of the country.

So, thanks to far-seeing men like Ned Irish, college basketball was really beginning to come of age. Irish was the first to realize that the sport no longer belonged in the dimly-lit bandbox gyms, lofts and river barges to which it had been relegated for so long. The answer was Madison Square Garden and doubleheader basketball, and the combination ushered in a whole new era.

41

The Big Men

To capitalize on the immediate success of the NIT, the NCAA quickly planned its own first tournament. There would be an eight-team field, each team representing a different region of the country. A selection committee was then appointed to choose the teams.

The pattern that emerged saw the NCAA inviting mostly teams affiliated with a conference, while the NIT tended to take independent teams. The result was two distinct tournaments, each with its own look and its share of outstanding ballclubs. And with this system, both events were able to field equally strong teams and to offer top-notch competition. It stayed that way for many years before the NCAA began to get recognition as *the* tournament, the one that resulted in the crowning of a national champion. But in the early years the equality of the two tournaments could only serve to strengthen the game and add to its continued growth.

The 1938-39 season saw the emergence of yet another powerhouse ballclub at Long Island University. Clair Bee had done it again, coaching his team through an unbeaten season. The Blackbirds were talented and deep, and Coach Bee had outstanding seniors in all-America Irv Torgoff, Danny Kaplowitz, Dolly King, George Newman

and Mike Sewitch. What made the team great, however, was that Bee had three sophomores who could come in without the team losing a beat. Ossie Shechtman, Solly Schwartz and Cy Lobello played beyond their years and made major contributions.

But the Blackbirds didn't complete their great season without adversity. For their final game of the regular season LIU had to travel to Convention Hall in Philadelphia to face LaSalle. Knowing the power of the Blackbirds, LaSalle went into a slowdown game, figuring it was the only way they had a chance to win. And somehow the Explorers managed to hold a small lead for most of the game, while LIU remained patient and waited for its chance. Then, late in the game, Johnny Bromberg of LIU was fouled. He stepped to the line with a chance to give the Blackbirds the lead. Suddenly, out of the blue, a LaSalle player walked over to Bromberg and punched him square in the nose.

Within seconds there was a near riot at Convention Hall. Fans charged out of the stands and attacked the LIU players, and it took a considerable time to clear the floor and allow the game to resume. LIU then showed its grit and went on to a 28-21 victory, but the Blackbirds had paid a price. The disgraceful show by LaSalle and its fans resulted

in a broken nose for Bromberg and, worse yet, a broken arm for Mike Sewitch. And now the banged-up Blackbirds had to enter the NIT tournament as favorites.

The biggest question now was whether the Blackbirds could overcome their injuries. Coach Bee felt that the team to beat would be undefeated Loyola of Chicago. It was a strong NIT field, but when the smoke cleared the final confrontation was, as Bee had predicted, LIU vs Loyola. The Chicago team had an outstanding big man in 6ft 8in Mike Novak, who was a fine shotblocker, and in those days goaltending was still legal, and a good big man could swat shots away even if they were coming down into the hoop.

Bee had his best shooters, Torgoff and Kaplowitz, practice banking their shots high off the backboard, where hopefully Novak couldn't reach them. And then he decided to gamble: he told Mike Sewitch to guard Novak. Sewitch still had his broken arm in a cast, but he readily agreed to guard the Loyola big guy.

As it turned out, Bee's strategy worked. Despite the broken arm, the burly Sewitch was able to force Novak away from the basket, keeping him away from the boards and allowing LIU to win the game 44-32. Torgoff led the way, with 12 points, while Kaplowitz and Shechtman had nine each in a game Clair Bee always called his greatest victory.

The first NCAA field was probably not as strong as the NIT's that year. There were no unbeaten teams chosen, the club with the best record being Oregon, at 26-5. The Ducks had an unusually tall team for 1939: Slim Wintermute, the center, stood 6ft 8in, and Laddie Gale and John Dick were a pair of 6ft 4½in forwards. Because they were usually taller than their opponents, Oregon fans nicknamed their front line "The Tall Firs."

Oregon had played a big 31-game schedule in 1938-39, which was unusual for that time, yet come tournament time the Ducks were ready. They made their way to the semifinals, where they easily

OPPOSITE: *Coach Clair Bee and his LIU Blackbirds in 1938.*

TOP: *Coach Howard Hobson (3rd from right, front row) and his University of Oregon team celebrate winning the first NCAA tournament in 1939. The Ducks topped Ohio State, 46-33, in the final.*

ABOVE: *An intense Clair Bee (left) instructs his Long Island team during a timeout. Throughout his long career Bee was considered to be one of the best coaches that the game of basketball had produced anywhere in the country.*

OPPOSITE: *Seton Hall's Bob Davies.*

LEFT: *Just one reason the 1939 Ducks were called the "Tall Firs."*

ABOVE: *John "Honey" Russell in his pro playing days. Russell later became a popular and remarkably successful coach at Seton Hall.*

defeated Oklahoma 55-37. Then they watched as Ohio State whipped Villanova of Philadelphia in the other semifinal 53-36. The Buckeyes, just 14-6 in the regular season, were clearly on a late roll. So now it was Oregon against Ohio State for the first-ever NCAA title. The game was played at the Patton Gym on the Northwestern University Campus in Evanston, Illinois, on March 27, 1939.

It was a good game, one with a surprising development. Though many people expected Oregon to win because of the dominance of the Tall Firs inside, the game took another twist. That was the exciting play of Oregon guard Bobby Anet, who stood just 5ft 8in. The little backcourt man played a superb game, his expert ballhandling leading the Ducks to a 21-16 halftime lead and a 46-33 NCAA victory. John Dick paced the winners by scoring with 15 points, while Anet added ten to go with his brilliant floor leadership. The NCAA had put on an exciting and successful first tournament.

Two events took place during the next season that symbolized both the past and future of basketball. On November 28, 1939, word came that James Naismith had died. The creator of the court game was 78 years old and had stayed active on the Kansas University faculty until two years prior to his death. He had lived long enough to witness the spread of his game to every part of the country, and he must have been proud.

The second milestone event took place on February 28, 1940. It was the first television broadcast ever of a basketball game. The station was then called W2XBS, but was actually a forerunner of WNBC in New York. Television equipment was set up at Madison Square Garden to air a doubleheader that had Pittsburgh playing Fordham and NYU going up against Georgetown. It was only an experiment, and the picture was lost intermittently during parts of both games, but it proved that the court game did lend itself to TV coverage and thus was

a kind of glimpse into a future when basketball would be nation-wide television favorite.

The same season saw both tournaments held successfully once again. Colorado was the NIT champ, defeating Duquesne in the final 51-40, while the NCAA champion was Indiana, winning their first title with a 60-42 win over Kansas. Yet to many, neither of these champion clubs was the best in the country. That honor, some said, should go to Seton Hall, the New Jersey school that had won 19 straight games in an unbeaten year. But for some reason, Seton Hall chose not to go to either tournament, so whether they would have won will always remain a matter of conjecture.

Seton Hall was coached by John "Honey" Russell, and he had put together a team of talented ballplayers. The club had played extremely well the season before, but it took a freak accident to bring it all together. The Pirates relied a great deal on their 6ft 7in center, Ed Sadowski. But near the end of the 1938-39 season Sadowski had broken his leg and was out. At that point Russell decided to go with five sophomores and create a running, ball-hawking team. With the five sophs the Pirates won their final four games that year, then came back even stronger the following year.

Bob Holm, John Ruthenberg, Ken Pine and Bob Fisher were good ballplayers, but it took a great ballplayer to make it all work. He was Bob Davies, a slick backcourt man and shooter who did everything superbly. Davies excited the crowds with his ball-handling wizardry, which featured a behind-the-back dribble á la Hank Luisetti. Indeed, Davies freely admitted that he loved to put on a show out there, to entertain the fans while playing winning basketball at the same time.

"I've always been grateful for Honey Russell letting me play the kind of game I wanted to play," Davis said as he looked back at his career. "I was starting to throw a lot of behind-the-back passes and dribbling behind my back. I didn't go out there with the intention of being fancy. It was just different ways to try to get the ball to someone. If you had to throw it behind your head or around your back, or some other way, you did it."

With the five sophomores returning as juniors in 1939-40, the club went unbeaten. Yet they didn't go to either of the post-season tourneys. But when the Pirates were again unbeaten in 1940-41, this time they accepted a bid to the NIT. There were eight teams in the field, and despite Seton Hall's 42-game winning streak, the co-favorites were Duquesne and Ohio University.

But Davies and his Pirates teammates won their first-round game against Rhode Island State 70-54, to run their winning streak to 43. Then, in the semifinals, the Pirates ran into another of Clair Bee's great LIU teams. Bee assigned Solly Schwartz to guard Davies, and the LIU veteran held the Seton Hall star scoreless in the first half. Davies finally fouled out, with some seven minutes remaining, after scoring just four points. LIU won easily 49-26 and reached the finals against Ohio University. With Schwartz getting 19 and Ossie Shechtman 12, the Blackbirds took the NIT crown with a 56-42 triumph.

In the NCAA tourney Big Ten-champ Wisconsin was the surprise winner. The Badgers were almost eliminated in the opening round by Dartmouth, as all-American Gus Broberg scored 20 for the Ivy Leaguers. But soph John Kotz hit two free throws in the closing seconds to cement a 51-50 win. From there, Wisconsin made it all the way to the finals, then won the title with a 39-34 triumph over Washington State. Big Gene Englund had 13 points, and tourney MVP Kotz 12, for the winners.

That game also marked the end of basketball's first fifty years. The sport had begun in a small Springfield gym with two peach baskets hooked to the balcony back in 1891, and in half a century it had come a long way. While it was now well on its way to joining baseball and football as major American sports, the best was still yet to come, and some of that best was just around the corner.

LEFT: *Honey Russell and his Seton Hall ballclub celebrate still another big victory. The Pirates were unbeaten in 1940 but decided against going to either of the postseason tournaments. Even so, many called them the best in the country.*

The War Years

By the time the 1941-42 season opened the Japanese had bombed Pearl Harbor and the nation was at war. World War II would have its effects on college basketball in the same way it would affect all the other sports. Many potential players would be in the service, so the ranks of the teams at home would often be depleted. But sports was also considered a welcome diversion to the stress of war, so everyone tried to keep going. Stanford University won the NCAA title in 1942, topping Dartmouth 53-38, as Howard Dallmar scored 15 points. The NIT crown went to West Virginia when the Mountaineers topped Western Kentucky 47-45.

It was also a year in which the more wide open game was producing some new scoring records. Stanley "Stutz" Modzelewski of Rhode Island State concluded his four-year career with 1730 points, topping the 1596 scored by Hank Luisetti six years earlier. And West Texas State's Price Brookfield set a new single-season scoring mark with 520 points.

So it was another good year, but in 1942-43 college basketball began to feel the affects of the war. Some schools were forced to drop their programs completely, while others were saved by the passage of a special rule to allow freshmen to play varsity ball for the first time. But a number of intersectional games were cancelled because of the restrictions put on travel during the war.

Yet while fans wondered just what kind of a product they would see on college courts during this mid-war year, very few realized that the 1942-43 season would produce two players who would change the face of the sport. One of them made his debut as a freshman at De Paul University, while the other entered his freshman year at Oklahoma A & M. Yet when rumors about the two players began circulating there was skepticism voiced in may places. These guys obviously couldn't play college-brand ball, critics sneered. Why not? Simple. Both 6ft 10in George Mikan and 7ft 0in Bob Kurland were too tall!

There had been some big men in the game already, but very few

RIGHT: *Veteran Coach Ray Meyer directed the DePaul Blue Demons right into the 1980s. It was the same Meyer who is given credit for making George Mikan the first of the great big men when Mikan was at DePaul in the 1940s.*

OPPOSITE TOP: *Coach Hank Iba and his Oklahoma A&M Aggies. The Aggies really put themselves on the map when seven-footer Bob "Foothills" Kurland joined the team.*

OPPOSITE BOTTOM: *Stan "Stutz" Modzeliewski was a member of Frank Keaney's running Rhode Islanders in the early 1940s. Stan later played pro ball for the old Baltimore Bullets, and it's their uniform he is wearing here.*

giants. And these two freshman were giants. In addition, they both were what would be called "projects" today, meaning they needed a lot of work to learn the game. And this, too, was in keeping with the popular conception of very tall basketball players, for none of the previous giants who had tried the game had shown any real agility or skill. Many had been slow, and some were downright clumsy. Worse, few had ever bothered to learn anything more than the bare fundamentals of the game. They were out there because of their size and nothing more.

At first there was little evidence that either Mikan or Kurland would be any different. Mikan was so nearsighted that he had to wear his glasses during games, yet another reason to doubt that he had much future. In fact, before enrolling at De Paul, the big guy had worked out at Notre Dame and had been told by the Irish coach, George Keogan, to go to De Paul because "you'll make a better scholar than a basketball player." Kurland, who was even taller, already had the nickname "Foothills" because his huge feet got tangled so often when he ran up and down the court.

There was another, perhaps more basic, reason why these very tall men needed so much work to become players: they simply hadn't begun playing the game early enough. Maybe it was because people had told them they couldn't play, or perhaps they were embarrassed about their size. At any rate, both Mikan and Kurland needed a great deal of work and coaches with an abundance of patience. Fortunately, both men had the drive and desire to become great players, and in Ray Meyer at De Paul and Hank Iba at Oklahoma A & M they had the perfect coaches.

"No matter where a tall guy went in those days there was always someone to tell him he couldn't do something," Mikan said, in later years. "So it took a great deal of determination for me to prove I could do anything anyone else could do."

49

OPPOSITE: *George Mikan looks like a man among boys as he towers over his own teammates and the Indiana State team during a 1945 game.*

RIGHT: *Mikan played above the rim while most other players of the time played below it. But the big guy stilled worked hard to become a great all-round player.*

At De Paul Mikan really had to start from scratch. Coach Meyer knew it would take time and work, and he decided to start the big guy working without a basketball. In fact, big George didn't even touch a ball for the first month under Meyer's tutelage.

"Coach Meyer had me jumping rope, doing a lot of figure eights, running around chairs, lifting weights, boxing, dancing, running with the track team, all kinds of things like that. I also did a lot of hand and eye coordination work and a lot of work on my legs."

Ray Meyer didn't want a one-dimensional player, either. If he was going to develop Mikan, he wanted to do it right. That meant a complete player who could play defense, rebound, run the court and shoot with either hand. That last part took a special amount of hard work, because Mikan was right handed and had never really tried to use his left hand for this kind of thing before. It took several years for the big guy to develop a shot from the left side, but it was worth the wait.

"Coach Meyer also taught me to keep the ball high," Mikan remembered. "A lot of big men back then used to bring the ball down to their knees and get tied up. And when I was in the pivot he wanted me to carry the ball with two hands whenever possible. Plus I would do everything else the other players did, whether they were guards or forwards, all kinds of dribbling and shooting. He made me do it all, and I really worked hard."

It wasn't much different for Kurland. An intelligent youngster who went to college for the express purpose of getting his education, Kurland went out for basketball almost as an afterthought. He couldn't have been too pleased when a rival coach tabbed him a "glandular goon" almost immediately. Yet he had the same kind of drive that Mikan had and worked very hard right from the beginning.

"I never had the type of strength that Mikan had," Kurland would say, "so I never developed the same kind of game with the sweeping hook shot. Rather, I learned how to work a defender into position and take a quick little jump-push shot."

Though Mikan and Kurland were the greatest of the big, there were others as well, such as 6ft 9in Harry Boykoff of St. John's who helped to change the game. Their presence soon led to another rule change that helped make the game better and more interesting. When the two big men first suited up, defensive players were still allowed to knock a shot away anytime before it reached the hoop. But both big guys had become so good at this that by 1945 the rule changed. Now players were prohibited from knocking the ball away once it started its downward path to the basket. If they did swat a downward shot, "goaltending" was called and the basket counted. It's the same rule that's in effect today.

Neither big man really made much of an impact during his freshman

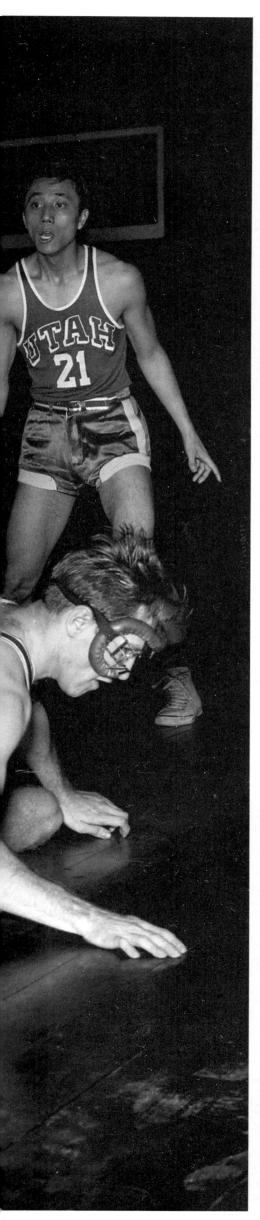

"We went into the NCAA Tournament without practicing and without a scouting report on the other teams," said Arnie Ferrin, who was the 18-year-old freshman star of the team. "We just went out there and played."

Maybe they were more relaxed than at the NIT, or maybe they were more determined. Whatever it was, the Utes suddenly looked like a different team. In the first round they defeated Missouri 45-35. Next they captured the West Championship, topping Iowa State 40-31. Now Ferrin and company found themselves in the finals against Dartmouth, the Eastern Champion. That, in itself, was quite an accomplishment, following the NIT debacle.

As a further irony, the title game had been scheduled for Madison Square Garden that year, the scene of the team's NIT loss. So the Utes headed back for New York, the city they had wanted to see in the first place. In the title game they were matched against the team from Dartmouth, and they found it a disconcertingly tough nut to crack. The game was close all the way. More than 15,000 fans cheered the fine all-around play of Ferrin and the great hustle of Utah's 5ft 7in guard, Wat Misaka. But it was Dartmouth's Dick McGuire who hit a half-court bank shot at the buzzer to tie the game at 36-all and give the NCAA its first overtime title game.

OPPOSITE: *The NCAA title game of 1944 was between a pair of unlikely teams. Utah topped Dartmouth 42-40 in a cliffhanger.*

ABOVE: *Utah star Arnie Ferrin tosses the ball to teammate Wat Misaka (21) during the 1944 title match with Dartmouth.*

BELOW: *It was trophy time for Coach Vadal Peterson and Utah after the Utes took the West Regional from Iowa State, 40-31, in 1944.*

LEFT: *Joe Lapchick and his St. John's Redmen celebrate their 1944 NIT championship at Madison Square Garden.*

BELOW LEFT: *Forrest "Phog" Allen, the longtime coach at Kansas, kept James Naismith's tradition alive at the Lawrence, Kansas, school.*

Utah hadn't come this far to lose. In the overtime session the 6ft 3in Ferrin took charge early, converting four free throws to put the Utes on top. But Dartmouth fought back again, and it took Herb Wilkinson's one-hander from the top of the key in the final seconds to seal a 42-40 championship victory for Utah. Ferrin was the tourney's MVP, but his team's Cinderella story wasn't over yet.

Like everyone else at this time, the people who ran college athletics were looking for ways to help the war effort. So they set up a special Red Cross benefit game between the two tournament winners, Utah and St. John's, the NIT champs. Once again the Garden was the scene, and this time some 18,000 fans crowded into the arena to watch the first game ever between the two tournament winners. Utah didn't disappoint. The Utes capped one of the greatest comebacks ever by topping the Redmen 43-36 and showing everyone that their NIT defeat was not really indicative of the team's talent.

By the next season the war would begin winding down, and basketball would be heating up. And for the next two years no one would dare to claim that either George Mikan nor Bob Kurland was too tall to play basketball. The two big guys dominated the college game. Even with the new rule against goal-tending in effect, the two giants still clogged the middle on defense, their very presence causing opposing players to change the trajectory of their shots and, as a result, often miss easy baskets.

From time to time there would be other attempts to diminish the advantage held by the big men. One early effort was made by Forrest "Phog" Allen, the longtime coach at Kansas. (Allen had taken over the Jayhawk coaching reins from none other than James Naismith in 1908.) Allen's idea was to raise the basket from ten to 12 feet. He tried it once in an experimental game, and 7ft 1in Elmore Merganthanler (not exactly a household name) of New Mexico State still scored 41 points. It was

OPPOSITE TOP: *Despite his greatness, George Mikan wasn't the only game in town. Here, Bowling Green's 6ft-11in Don Otten scores on the big guy during NIT action in 1945. Still, DePaul won the game 71-54, as Mikan tallied 34.*

OPPOSITE BOTTOM: *Mikan took home a lot of hardware during his DePaul days. This one was for being the NIT's Most Valuable Player in 1945.*

To some, Mikan's play was surprising. Though an extremely strong player inside, big George was not very fast. Also, his eyeglasses gave him something of a scholarly appearance, but then, four of the De Paul starters that year wore glasses, and one of them was only 16 years old. Nevertheless, Ray Meyer had put together a team that was very tough to beat.

There was an added motivation when it came time for the semifinal game against Rhode Island State. State's coach, Frank Keaney, was at it again. He boasted that his running, gunning ballclub would "drive Mikan nuts" with its fastbreaking, swarming attack. For good measure he added that the quickness of his team would have the big guy "stumbling over his own feet." And he finished his gasconade to the press by predicting that Mikan would go back to Chicago "with his tongue hanging out before we're through with him."

All Ray Meyer had to do was repeat Keaney's words before gametime. The unsmiling Blue Demons came onto the court like a team with a mission. They immediately took their attack right to their opponents and had the Rhode Island State team on the defensive all night. Mikan also played inspired ball, and when the game ended the Blue Demons had a one-sided 97-53 victory. Nor was that all. George Mikan had singlehandedly matched the entire scoring output of the Rhode Island State team. The big guy had exploded for 53 points, sending the Garden crowd home knowing they had just seen one of basketball's all-time greats.

The question now was whether the Blue Demons had peaked too soon. They still had to meet Bowling Green in the finals, and the Falcons had a good big man of their own in 6ft 11in Don Otten. De Paul did get caught napping at the gate as the Falcons burst out to an 11-0 lead, but before long Mikan and his teammates had things under control and came home a 71-54 winner to take the NIT crown. Mikan had finished this one with 34 more points and was a unanimous choice at the tournament's Most Valuable Player.

then that people began to realize that no matter how high you put the basket, the big men would still be the closest to it.

Mikan and Kurland went on dominating the scene in 1944-45. Big George led the nation in scoring, and both were first-team All-Americans. But because the NCAA selection committee usually picked its midwest representative from the Big Ten, De Paul opted to go to the NIT. Kurland and Oklahoma A & M would be going to the NCAA championships. So the two big men wouldn't be meeting in post-season play.

Or so it seemed until it was announced that there would be another Red Cross game between the two tournament champions. Thus if both the Blue Demons and Aggies won, the giants would indeed meet once more. Mikan wasted no time showing that he and his teammates were headed for that game. In the opening round of the NIT they came out and smoked West Virginia 76-52, as the big guy with number 99 on his jersey scored 33 points, much to the delight of the large Garden crowd.

ABOVE: *Hank Iba and the Oklahoma A&M Aggies celebrate the national championship in 1945, as NCAA Commissioner Tug Wilson presents the trophy. Between commissioner and coach stands big Bob Kurland, the team's star.*

RIGHT: *Bob Kurland chases North Carolina's "Bones" McKinney in 1946. Like Mikan, Bob Kurland worked very hard to become a complete player.*

OPPOSITE: *When the two giants met it was a real struggle. Here, Mikan goes high to block a Kurland shot during a 1946 game at Chicago Stadium.*

Now all eyes swung to the NCAA tourney to see if Kurland and his Oklahoma A & M teammates could duplicate De Paul's success. The Aggies got a break in the first round when they met defending champion Utah. The Utes had been depleted by the loss of All-American Arnie Ferrin and of Fred Sheffield to the military, and Oklahoma won handily, 62-37 Kurland scoring 28 points. In the semifinals the Aggies had little trouble with Arkansas, winning 68-41, and now they were headed to the finals. A championship would also put them into the Red Cross game against Mikan and De Paul.

The title game was set for Madison Square Garden, and that would enable the New York fans to compare the two giants. The Aggies would also be meeting a home-town team, as New York University had made its way to the finals. NYU had an All-American in Sid Tannenbaum, as well as an up-and-coming young center, 6ft 8in freshman Dolph Schayes, who would later go on to a storied career in the NBA.

With the huge Garden crowd urging them on, NYU played the Aggies tough. But Iba used a slowdown strategy to negate the Violets' fastbreak and also slow down Tannenbaum, who managed just four points. And while the Aggie defense did its job, Kurland found time to score 22 points at the other end and lead his club to a 49-45 victory and their first-ever NCAA crown. It came as no surprise when Kurland, who had scored a record 65 points in the three games, was named the tourney's MVP. And now the dream matchup with De Paul would take place, right there in the Garden.

More than 18,000 fans jammed into the big arena, contributing more than $50,000 to the Red Cross effort. But the game, which had been anticipated for so long, was something less than an artistic success. The two giants both got in foul trouble early. Mikan then fouled out after just 14 minutes and scored only nine points. Kurland hung in there the whole way, but tallied just 14, not even high for his team. The bottom line was that Oklahoma A & M won the game 52-44, prompting

Bob Kurland to call it "the game" of his college career.

But the two big guys had yet another year of collegiate eligibility remaining. With the war over, the 1945-46 season would unquestionably provide Mikan and Kurland with one more test. All the colleges would be at full strength again, but it would be the same two men who dominated the scene. Mikan and his De Paul teammates compiled a 19-5 record, with the big guy in the middle topping the nation in scoring average, shooting at more than a 23 point-per-game clip. Surprisingly, the Blue Demons declined to defend their NIT championship.

Kurland and Oklahoma A & M played an expanded schedule of 30 games, winning 28 of them. En route, Kurland set a new record of 643 points in a season, although many observers felt he was hampered by Coach Iba's slowdown style of play. That may very well have been true, for in the final game of the season against St. Louis University, Iba turned his charges loose, and the players decided to get the ball inside to the big guy. Kurland responded with a 58-point performance.

After that the Aggies set about defending their NCAA title. In the first game Kurland scored 20 in a 44-29 defeat of Baylor. Then, in the semifinals, Foothills popped for 29, as his club topped California easily, 52-35. Now it was back to the Garden for the title game against North Carolina, a team led by forward John Dillion and a thin 6ft 6in center named Horace "Bones" McKinney.

What looked like an easy win for A & M turned into a real struggle, as McKinney played Kurland tough most of the way. In the second half, first McKinney then Kurland fouled out. The game then came

BELOW: *It was trophy time again for Oklahoma A&M after a second straight NCAA title in 1946. The Aggies topped the North Carolina team 43-40.*

OPPOSITE: *Instead of playing pro ball, Bob Kurland took a job with the Phillips Petroleum Corp. and starred for the AAU Phillips 66ers for many years.*

down to the final seconds, when A & M prevailed 43-40, giving Hank Iba's team a second straight NCAA crown. Kurland had 23 points in the game, 72 for the tourney, and was once again the MVP.

Thus, after four years, the college careers of George Mikan and Bob Kurland came to an end. While the pro game beckoned to both stars, only one went. Mikan joined the Minneapolis Lakers and had a distinguished professional career in which he helped shape the future of the pro game as he had the college version. Kurland, on the other hand, decided not to become a professional. Instead, he began a business career with the Phillips Petroleum Corporation, advancing within

the company while playing AAU ball for the company team, the Phillips 66ers. He also participated in a pair of Olympic squads, adding two gold medals to his already large collection or hardware.

Thanks to Mikan and Kurland the college game had grown and matured. It was a bigger game than ever now, with bigger and better players coming in each year. No longer would coaches and fans look askance at a big guy. Mikan and Kurland had taken the too-tall theory and put it out to pasture, and because of their success other big guys would begin playing earlier, learning the game as kids and coming to college ready to make an immediate contribution to the sport.

PART III

Triumphs
and
Tragedies

But it was a battle. With Tucker playing very well, Oklahoma took a 31-28 lead into the locker room at halftime. Then Holy Cross fought back behind Kaftan. The Crusaders reclaimed the lead, but the Sooners stayed right on their heels. With just three minutes left it was still anyone's game at 48-45, Holy Cross up by three. But suddenly the Crusaders turned it on and opened it up for a 58-47 victory, making them the first school from the Northeast to take an NCAA title. Kaftan had scored 18 and was named the tourney's Most Valuable Player.

In the NIT that year it looked like another Kentucky victory. The Wildcats had won it the year before and now had Alex Groza at center, joining Ralph Beard and Wah Wah Jones. The team was still young, but they were nevertheless talented and relentless under the guiding hand of The Baron, Adolph Rupp. But the NIT was about to write something of a Cinderella story as well. Kentucky had defeated LIU 66-62, and North Carolina State 60-42, to reach the finals. The surprise was the team that was waiting to meet the Wildcats.

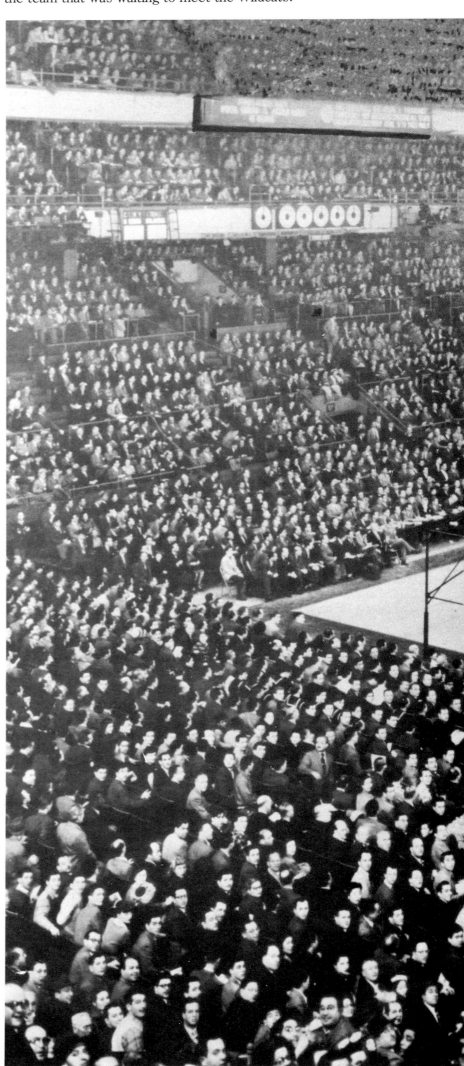

ABOVE: *This is how Bob Cousy looked as a Holy Cross freshman in 1947. The Cooz went on to become a pro great.*

RIGHT: *It was standing room only at Madison Square Garden when Holy Cross defeated Oklahoma for the NCAA title in 1947.*

It was the Utah Utes, the NCAA champs of 1944. Utah hadn't been expected to be much of a factor in the 1946-47 season until they got the good news that former all-American Arnie Ferrin was rejoining the team after a stint in the service. The club also had another outstanding player in Vern Gardner, who had been in the service back in '44 when the club was champion. In the preliminary rounds the Utes had squeezed by Duquesne, 45-44, and West Virginia, 64-62. But no one really thought they could beat Kentucky.

The Utes entered the game as 11-point underdogs, but, as had been the case three years earlier, little Wat Misaka came up big, holding Ralph Beard to just a single free throw. At the same time, Gardner and Ferrin had 15 points apiece, to lead the Utes to a big upset victory of 49-45 and send Adolph Rupp back to Lexington to lick his wounds.

Losing was something The Baron could never accept. He ran his program with an iron hand, believing strongly in discipline, in having a second-nature knowledge of the fundamentals of the game and in fol-

ABOVE: *Adolph Rupp's powerful Kentucky team won a pair of NCAA titles in 1948 and '49. Led by center Alex Groza (15), guard Ralph Beard (12) and forward Wah Wah Jones (27), this was one of the greatest Wildcat teams ever. Coach Rupp is seated on the left in the front row.*

RIGHT: *Utah won the 1947 NIT title with a 49-45 upset win over Kentucky. The happy Utes, from left, include Vern Gardner and Arnie Ferrin. Gardner is accepting the Outstanding Player trophy from John F. Coffey (right).*

OPPOSITE: *George Kafton of Holy Cross gets a hero's ride after leading Holy Cross to the 1947 NCAA title, a 58-47 win over Oklahoma. The all-American Kafton was also the tourney's MVP.*

lowing his own instincts for tactics and strategy. And once he began getting top players, his teams were tough to stop. He drilled his team incessantly behind closed doors. To Rupp the gym was a classroom, and he wouldn't put up with interruptions. Yet as much as he loved basketball and wanted to win, he also urged his players to study and get their educations. Any player who wavered from his studies *or* from his hoop was sure to get into trouble with the veteran coach, who once said the only fun comes when you put the trophy in the trophy case. And the case was bulging at Kentucky.

The 1947-48 Wildcat team was undoubtedly a great one. Alex Groza, the 6ft 7in center, had become the focal point of attack. Groza had come to Lexington as a freshman in 1945, but he had gone into the service, and when he returned he was stronger and more mature. In Wallace "Wah Wah" Jones Rupp had a tough and reliable forward. Ralph Beard was the quarterback, a cat-quick guard who was getting better and better. Cliff Barker and Ken Rollins may have been the forgotten starters, but both were competent ballplayers molded into playing a particular role by their coach. Together they formed a starting Wildcat team that became known as the Fabulous Five. But what made the Wildcats even greater was that Rupp also had a deep bench. He could rest his starters and never worry about losing too much on the court. That was the way the coach wanted it: he felt a team couldn't have enough good players.

One example of the kind of perfectionist coach The Baron had become could be seen in a game against Arkansas when the Wildcats seemingly could do no wrong. By halftime Kentucky had an almost unbelievable 38-4 lead, and the players were pretty much laughing it up when Rupp entered the locker room. His players could see right away that their coach wasn't happy, but they couldn't figure out why. Suddenly The Baron erupted and demanded to know who was guarding the Arkansas player who had scored his team's only field goal.

ABOVE: *The Most Valuable Player in the 1948 NCAA tournament was Kentucky's Alex Groza. Though just 6ft-7in, Groza was an extremely quick center and was often nearly unstoppable underneath.*

OPPOSITE: *Easy Ed Macauley was a smooth 6ft-8in forward with St. Louis University in the late 1940s. Easy Ed's effortless style also made him an NBA star with both Boston and St. Louis.*

"I had him," said one of the Kentucky players.

"Well, you had better get on him," yelled Rupp. "He's running wild out there!"

Rupp was one of those coaches for whom no lead was ever safe, no game was ever won until the final buzzer. But for all his crotchets he was an inspired coach. His 1945-46 club, with freshmen Beard and Jones, was 28-2 and took the NIT. With Groza back the next season, the Wildcats were 34-3. And even though they were upset in the NIT by Utah, the club was obviously one of the very best in the country. So it came as no surprise when the team was every bit as good in 1947-48. They ripped through the regular season, winning 29 and losing just two, both of those by a single point. This time they decided to go to the NCAA.

And they made it look easy. In the opening round they topped Columbia 76-53. Next came Holy Cross, where Bob Cousy was beginning to emerge as a great player. But neither the Cooz or his talented teammates could tame Kentucky, and the Wildcats won again, 60-52. The championship game was set against Baylor, and it was really no contest. Groza popped in 14 points, and Beard 12, as the Wildcats took the crown 58-42. With Groza the tourney MVP, the basketball world had to accept the fact that the entire group would be back for an encore the following season.

OPPOSITE: *More and more great players were entering the college ranks in the late 1940s. Here, NYU's Dolph Schayes battles for the ball against St. Louis as Easy Ed Macauley moves in from behind.*

RIGHT: *NIT action in 1949 produced a huge upset when Loyola of Chicago upended mighty Kentucky 67-56. Here, Loyola center Jack Kerris gets a joyous ride, but the true nature of the upset wasn't known until a few years later.*

St. Louis University won the NIT that year behind 24 points by Easy Ed Macauley, who would go on to a great pro career. The Billikens defeated Dolph Schayes and NYU 65-52 for the title. While the NIT would certainly continue to be an important post-season tournament for many more years, the NCAA event was gradually taking on greater significance. It would eventually be the stage upon which a national champion was crowned at the end of each season, but at this time an NIT win was still equally prestigious and would display some great basketball drama over the next several years.

The 1948-49 season brought a couple of additional changes to the college basketball world. For one thing, it was the first year of the Associated Press poll. The weekly ratings showed teams just how they were ranked, at least in the minds of the writers. And there was

also a new rule that permitted coaches to talk with their teams during timeouts. Before that, the players would just sit on the court during a timeout, but now the rule committee had made it possible to put more strategy into the game by allowing coaches to tell their teams what they were doing wrong, set up plays or change defensive assignments. It was an overdue innovation.

But while changes may have improved the overall game, nothing could stop the Kentucky juggernaut. The Wildcats did suffer an early-season upset at the hands of Ed Macauley and St. Louis, 42-40, but that might even have helped the team, for after the defeat Rupp decided to have his offense concentrate on working the ball inside to Groza, who had become a strong and dominant player. Thereafter the Wildcats rolled, winning 21 straight. They compiled a perfect 13-0

LEFT: *The 1948 NIT title was won by St. Louis. More and more schools were now fielding outstanding basketball teams led by fine individual stars*

mark in Southeastern Conference play, and when the regular season ended the club had lost only the single game to St. Louis and was ranked number one in the AP poll.

With the tournaments approaching, Rupp had another idea: he wanted his Wildcats to become the first team to win both the NIT and NCAA crowns in the same season. The way the tournaments were set up then, it was possible, and sure enough, the Wildcats received bids to both events and were immediately installed as favorites.

They first went to the NIT, for what was expected to be a relatively easy game against Loyola of Illinois. But suddenly things went wrong. The Wildcats couldn't seem to sustain their attack, and when the game ended they had been not only beaten, but shocked, 61-56. "We were flat and dead," said Rupp, still trying to figure out what had happened. It would take a couple of years to find out, and it would be a game that would come back to haunt Rupp, as well as Alex Groza and Ralph Beard.

But the Baron didn't want to see his team's great season to go entirely by the board. There was still the NCAA tournament the following week, and the coach went about getting his team ready. When they took the court for the opening round game against Villanova the Wildcats showed they were back. They topped the Philadelphia school easily, 85-72, then had a second easy game against Illinois, winning by a 76-47 score. Now it was onto the finals, where Kentucky and Rupp would be meeting Oklahoma A & M, coached by another legend, Hank Iba.

Iba had restructured his team after losing Bob Kurland to graduation, but he still played his slow, ball-control game. And because he felt it was the only way he could beat the high-flying Wildcats, he slowed the pace even more. The result wasn't the most exciting game in the world, but, with Groza doing the damage on the inside, Kentucky won it 46-36, for its second straight NCAA crown. Groza had scored 25 points in the final, to take yet another MVP prize. "I guess

ABOVE: *The Groza- and Beard-led Kentucky team picked up the NCAA hardware again in 1949. Coach Rupp, center, once said that his teams got their fun when they put the trophy in the trophy case. And there were plenty of trophies for the Baron's Wildcat teams.*

LEFT: *By the late 1940s Nat Holman was building a powerhouse at City College (CCNY). Here, in a strategy session, the veteran coach talks with (front row from left) Norm Mager, Joe Galiber, Irwin Dambrot, Mike Wittlin and Ed Roman. In the rear are Ed Warner, Al Roth, Seymour Levy and Herb Cohen.*

OPPOSITE: *Nat Holman brought competitiveness, teaching ability and leadership to his CCNY teams. Here he jokes with three of his 1950 players. By the time the season ended, CCNY would have all of New York smiling.*

we vindicated ourselves," Rupp told the New York Press after his club's Madision Square Garden triumph.

Groza, Beard and Jones were all UPI first-team All-Americans and were joined by Macauley and Tony Lavelli of Yale. The AP ledger had high-scoring Vince Boryla of Denver replacing Jones on the first team. But it had certainly been a Wildcat year. And in an unprecedented move, the National Basketball Association took Groza, Beard and Jones and put them into a new NBA franchise, the Indianapolis Olympians, a team made up of many former Kentucky players. The team would win its division in its first year in the league, with Groza second in league scoring to the one and only George Mikan. So the Kentucky trio seemed headed for great pro careers. But that Loyola game still had to be explained.

Then came 1949-50, a season that would make college basketball history. The first great memory of the season was provided by the City College of New York team. For that year CCNY, under Coach Nat Holman, did what Adolph Rupp and Kentucky had tried to accomplish the season before: they captured both the NIT and NCAA championships, the first and only time that has been done in college basketball history.

The story begins with the coach. Nat Holman had always been a big basketball name around New York. He had been a pioneer player in the pro game, a member of the Original Celtics, the most famous of the early pro teams. And they were as successful as they were famous. Though the Celtics had many fine players in those early days, Nat Holman was always a driving force. He was not a big man, but he was a fiery competitor who played the game all out, no matter how rough or how badly bruised he became.

Because he loved to teach the game as well as play it, Holman decided to double up, and he became CCNY's head coach in 1920, even though he was still in his prime as a player. He continued in this dual role right through to 1949-50, juggling his schedule, sometimes rushing from a game as a player to the game he had to coach. It wasn't easy, but Holman loved it and did both jobs very well.

City College was somewhat different from most schools. There was no tuition, so only the best students could gain entrance. Most of the top basketball players from the New York City area were not top students and therefore tended to go elsewhere. That left Nat Holman with the problem of trying to scour up whatever talent was left behind and to build his program from there.

There was a period before World War II when the CCNY program seriously faltered. Holman had his own ideas about basketball, and some of them just didn't keep up with the times. For instance, he taught a highly-disciplined, short-passing game that was not unlike the game played by the Original Celtics. For awhile that worked, but when the college game began to open up Holman and his teams got left beyond, and because the coach wouldn't change, the program suffered through a number of losing seasons. But after the war Holman gradually saw the light. He began producing teams that could run and fast-break, and he also began allowing his players to shoot one-handed. Soon thereafter CCNY began to win again.

At the outset of the 1949-50 season Holman's ballclub consisted of one senior starter and four sophomores. The senior was 6ft 4in forward Irwin Dambrot, and he was joined by 6ft 2in Ed Warner, who also played up front, by 6ft 6in center Ed Roman and by a pair of 6ft 3in guards, Al Roth and Floyd Layne. Holman thought that it might take

RIGHT: *A team picture to end all team pictures. This one was taken after Nat Holman and his CCNY ballclub made history by becoming the only team to win both the NCAA and NIT titles in the same year (1950).*

another season for his sophomores to mature as players, but when the ballclub won 13 of its first 15 games it began to look as if the future was now. But in the final weeks of the season the team let down and only won four of its final seven games. That gave the Beavers a 17-5 mark for the year: good, but below everyone's expectations after the fast start.

Holman didn't think his team would get a bid to either post-season tournament, and normally he would have been right. But the NIT had expanded to 12 teams, and the selection committee was having some problems filling all the spots. Finally, with just one spot left, the committee figured it might as well opt for a local team to ensure more fan interest, CCNY got the final bid, and they jumped at it.

First up was San Francisco, the defending champion. For this one Holman reverted to a slowdown game, the Dons' usual style, and he beat them at their own game. Warner got hot and scored 26 points, as the Beavers made it look easy, 65-46. Next came Kentucky. Adolph Rupp had lost his superstars from the year before, but he had built his latest club around a 7ft 0in sophomore name Bill Spivey and had surprised everyone with a 25-4 mark. Once again CCNY was the underdog.

This time Holman went to the running game, and the City College

speed, crisp passing and fastbreak basketball beat the young Wildcats handily. Kentucky just didn't have the same kind of talent to run with the New York club, and CCNY ran them into the ground, 89-50. It was one of the biggest losses in Kentucky basketball annals, and it got many fans to thinking about the Beavers as possible NIT champs. Warner had scored 26 more, while Dambrot had 20 and Roman 17. And when the club upset Duquesne 62-52 they found themselves in the finals against the Bradley Braves.

Bradley wouldn't be easy. The Braves had a sound team and a pair of All Americans, Paul Unruh and Gene "Squeaky" Melchiorre. And to add to the Beavers' problems, Coach Holman had been sick with a high fever, and there was a question as to whether he would be able to attend the game. That worry, at least, ended when he arrived just before it began.

The game was a close one. Bradley had the early lead, and Holman decided his club had better slow the pace. The change in strategy worked, and the Beavers slowly fought their way back. With just two minutes left they had a 64-61 lead. Bradley then began to foul, but CCNY made their shots and controlled several jump balls, finally winning the tournament with a 69-61 victory. Great as this was, the Beavers weren't through yet.

LEFT: In a strange twist, CCNY had to play Bradley in the finals of both tournaments, and Nat Holman's ballclub won both times with the kind of fierce play shown here.

OPPOSITE: CCNY's double triumph was a joyous occasion for Nat Holman and the rest. But just over the horizon lay college basketball's first and worst scandal, a nearly disastrous event that put the integrity of the whole sport in question. And the champion CCNY team would not escape the stain.

Because the NIT was always played a week before the NCAA tourney, teams could conceivably participate in both. And, possibly because the Beavers had won the NIT, they received a belated bid to the NCAA. Now CCNY had a chance to win the unprecedented double. They had to work hard, but the Beavers won a squeaker over Ohio State, 56-55, and another close one against North Carolina State, 78-73. Now they had reached the final round, and by a strange twist of fate their opponents would again be the Bradley Braves. Bradley, too, had gotten a late bid, and the Braves wanted nothing better than to show CCNY that their NIT victory had been a fluke. So after victories over UCLA and Baylor, Bradley was ready to do battle with Holman's club once again at Madison Square Garden.

The game was much like the NIT final, close and hard-fought. The lead kept changing hands in the early going before CCNY began asserting itself. The Beavers made the first break and took a 39-32 lead into the locker room at halftime. But the Braves wouldn't quit. In the closing minutes they went into a full court press, and it began to bother the Beavers. Relentlessly Bradley cut the lead to just a point, at 69-68.

With time running out Gene Melchiorre stole the ball and headed upcourt. This was the crucial moment.

Melchiorre tried to take the shot himself. But Irwin Dambrot came out of nowhere to block it. The ball went to City's Norm Mager, who went all the way in for a layup to clinch the game, the title and the double win at 71-68. CCNY had added the NCAA crown to its NIT title, thus accomplishing what a great Kentucky team could not the season before. And they had done it all on their home court of Madison Square Garden. Nothing could have been finer. An ecstatic Nat Holman said afterward, "It took us an hour to play each game, but it will take a lifetime to forget them."

A lifetime to forget! They were almost prophetic words, but unfortunately for the wrong reason. College basketball had boomed after World War II, with more great players coming down the pike every year, more teams building programs and both the NIT and NCAA tournaments growing in popularity and prestige. But just around the corner lurked big trouble, the kind of trouble that would come close to undoing everything that college basketball had so far achieved.

Scandal

ABOVE: *Manhattan's Junius Kellogg shows his feeling about being offered a bribe to perform at less than his best. He reported the offer to Coach Ken Norton, who went to the police.*

The basketball world was still talking about the CCNY double victory when people began hearing stories to the effect that something was going on beneath the surface of college game, and once rumors start, people investigate. Yet the game still seemed on top of the world. The All America team in 1950 included future pro stars such as Bob Cousy of Holy Cross, Bill Sharman of Southern California, Dick Schnittker of Ohio State and Paul Arizin of Villanova. What could go wrong?

The answer was plenty, and the rumors became even louder after the 1950-51 season had begun. Specifically, the rumors involved gambling, and when you talk about gambling in sports, you're raising questions about the fix.

People have, of course, always made bets on the outcome of sporting events. Betting on a contest between individuals and teams in something that occurs in places as diverse as the family living room, the back alley or via a surreptitious call to the bookmaker. Everyone knows that these forms of gambling exist, but the presence of bookmakers and big-time gamblers around athletes had necessarily been a major concern for those who worry about the integrity of our games.

Whenever people speak of sports and gambling the first thing that usually comes to mind is the infamous "Black Sox" scandal of 1919. That happened as a result of a group of gamblers attempting to fix the 1919 World Series between the Chicago White Sox and Cincinnati Reds. Several members of the Sox were offered money to throw the Series to the underdog Reds. The plot was discovered after the deed was done, and the eight players implicated were banned from baseball for life. But the scandal still gave the game of baseball a blemish that hung over the sport for many years.

By the 1940s betting on college basketball games among spectators and fans was widespread. Not only would people bet on which team

OPPOSITE TOP: *New York District Attorney Frank Hogan thanks George Washington's Dave Shapiro for reporting a bribe attempt that led to the arrest of four men on charges of trying to "fix" a Madison Square Garden game in January 1949.*

OPPOSITE RIGHT: *In February of 1951 Eddie Gard, who was captain of the 1950 LIU team, appeared in court after admitting he offered a bribe to three players on the CCNY team.*

would win or lose, they also bet on a pre-set point spread. This system allowed people to bet on an underdog and still have a chance to win. For example, it the spread was seven points, the favorite would have to win the game by more than seven for those betting on that team to collect. If the favorite won the game, but by less than the seven-point spread, then those betting on the underdog would win. In other words, it was possible to make big money on a team that came up the loser in the box score.

With this kind of system firmly in place it was no real surprise that gamblers took it one step further. All that was needed was for a couple of players on one of the stronger teams to help out just a little. They wouldn't have to throw a game: all they would have to do was make sure their team didn't cover the spread. It might mean a missed free throw, a blown layup, an errant pass – things a good player could do easily without looking too obvious. And he wouldn't be costing his team a victory, just "shaving" the few points to enable his team to come in under the spread. That way he could pick up a few bucks and the gamblers could make a fortune.

This kind of thinking created a scenerio in which sooner or later some players would be approached. With so many ballplayers coming from poor environments, from families that could use a few dollars, there were enough kids gullible enough, or wiseguy enough, to go for the deal. Plus their teams would still win the games. Who could really get hurt?

Rumors of point shaving had been heard on and off during the early 1940s. The rumors became reality in 1945, when it was reported that five members of the Brooklyn College team had taken $1000 apiece to intentially lose a Madison Square Garden game with Akron College. The story broke after a Brooklyn College starter named Bill Rosenblatt refused to cooperate with the scheme. When school and Garden authorities heard the story they promptly cancelled the game rather than take a chance on a fix. Later, two men were caught and convicted of offering the players money. They received a year in jail, and the players involved were all expelled from school.

But anyone who knew human nature should have known that it wouldn't end there. One longtime coach who had felt that Madison Square Garden was full of potential for these kinds of shenanigans was Phog Allen of Kansas. But despite the respect the longtime coach had in the basketball community, his warnings and those of others were

generally ignored. But isolated incidents kept cropping up. In 1949 a member of the George Washington University team said that he had been approached by gamblers about throwing a game as well as playing with the point spread. Again there were arrests, this time by New York City District Attorney Frank Hogan. Sure enough, the four men arrested were all known gamblers, and they wound up serving short prison terms for their fix attempt.

But how much could really be done to stop gambling at big city arenas such as Madison Square Garden? Point spreads were public knowledge, often appearing in the newspapers and on the radio. There wasn't a coach or a player going into a big game who didn't know about the point spread. In fact, in the closing minutes of some ballgames it became obvious that many of the fans were rooting more for the point spread than for the win-lose outcome. It seemed just a matter of time before something really unpleasant happened. It did, all right, during the first few weeks of 1951. And the ensuing investigation quickly mushroomed into a scandal beyond anyone's worst fears. Every day there seemed to be new revelations about dirty doings, and people began to wonder just how widespread the whole thing had become. College basketball, which had grown so rapidly and so steadily for more than half a century, was in big trouble.

The whole thing began to unravel when Junius Kellogg, who played for Manhattan College, went to his coach, Ken Norton, and reported that he had been offered $1000 if he could make sure that his team lost its upcoming game with De Paul by at least ten points. The thing that really shocked Kellogg was that the offer came from one of the Jaspers' co-captains of the year before. Kellogg had also been told that the former player and another of his teammates had thrown three games during the previous season and had made $5000 in the process. He had bragged about not being caught.

Kellogg, who was the first black player at Manhattan, reported the bribe offer because he didn't want to jeopardize himself or his family. Coach Norton, sensing the seriousness of the situation, went im-

ABOVE: *Both Ed Roman (left) and Ed Warner of the champion CCNY team were charged with accepting bribes. They are shown here just after being released on $15,000 bail in February 1951.*

RIGHT: *CCNY's Al Roth looked a long way from his glory days when he, too, was implicated in the growing scandal in February of 1951.*

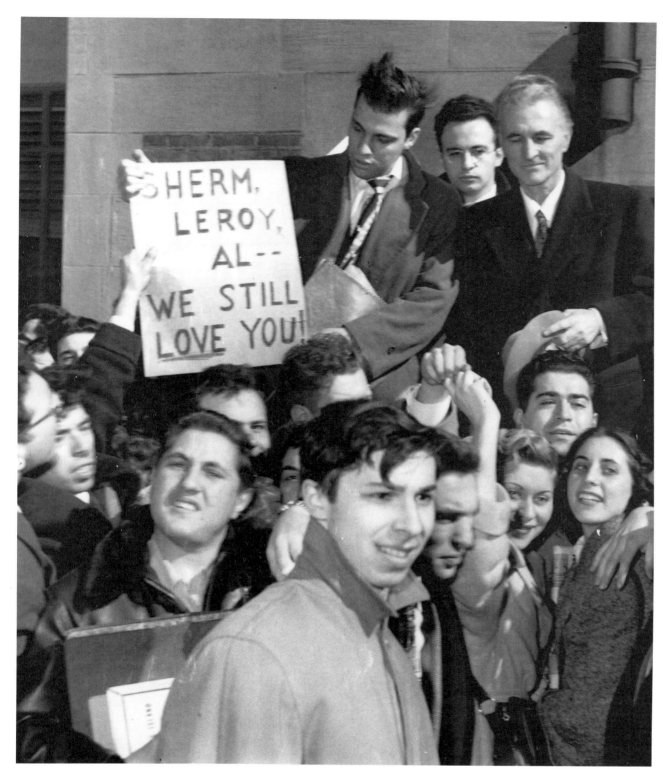

LEFT: *LIU Coach Clair Bee (standing right) joins a student rally to protest the suspension of major sports at the University. The names on the sign refer to LIU players Sherman White, Leroy Smith and Adolph Bigos, all named in the scandal.*

BELOW: *Salvatore Sollazzo (center) was charged with bribing college players to fix games at Madison Square Garden. The jewelry manufacturer was indicted on 13 counts by a Grand Jury in March 1951.*

mediately to the Manhattan district attorney's office. Manhattan won the game in question, but the gamblers and two former players were arrested.

"I'm shocked by all this," said Coach Norton. "I had no idea this was happening on my team last year. I knew the kids weren't doing so well, but it never occurred to me that they were throwing games."

The strange part was that even with the Manhattan situation staring them in the face, college authorities still didn't act as quickly as they might have. Maybe most of them still hoped the whole thing would go away, or simply that their own schools wouldn't be involved. But that would have been too easy.

A short time later veteran sportswriter and editor Max Kase of the New York *Journal American* was told an amazing story by a known bookmaker. The man told him of a former college star who was then acting as a go-between for known gamblers. His job was to approach players and try to talk them into taking bribes. Ignoring his journalistic instinct to save the scoop for his own paper, Kase instead went directly to District Attorney Hogan and told him what he had heard. That led to a full-scale investigation that blew the lid off the entire sport.

The result of the probe revealed that some 86 games in 23 cities had been fixed between 1947 and 1950 by 32 players from seven colleges. The schools named in the investigation were LIU, NYU, Manhattan, Bradley, Toledo and two real surprise blockbusters . . . Kentucky and CCNY! News of the first five was tough enough to take, but the last

two were almost unthinkable. CCNY was just a few short months re-moved from its amazing double victory in the NIT and NCAA tourna-ments, while the Kentucky team seemed under the total control of Adolph Rupp, who had publicly said of the gamblers that "they couldn't touch my boys with a ten-foot pole."

But once the first few arrests were made, and a few players began to talk, the domino effect quickly took over, and the shock waves re-verberated throughout the college basketball world. One of the first arrested was Eddie Gard, a former LIU player who had been the one acting as a go-between to recruit players to work with the gamblers. Gard, in fact, had been the first to reach Nat Holman's CCNY team. The ballclub was returning from an early-season game with Temple when Coach Holman was informed that three of his players would be met at the train station by representatives of the DA's office. All the veteran coach could tell his players was to tell the truth.

CCNY starters Ed Roman, Al Roth and Ed Warner finally did tell the truth, but only after hours of intense questioning. And when they began to talk the sordid story of what had happened began to emerge, for the players confessed that they had taken money to throw three games during the 1949-50 season. Suddenly it became clear just why CCNY had suffered that mysterious late-season slump that almost prevented the team from going to the post-season tournaments and making history.

Eddie Gard, apparently, was working for a man named Salvatore Sollazzo, a jewelry manufacturer and former convict. Gard made his contacts during the summer months when hundreds of players would make an annual trip to the Catskill Mountains, where they would play for the various resort hotels in the summer leagues. The object was to wine and dine the players, give them a taste of the good life, then offer them even more.

It started with Gard and an LIU teammate in 1950, when they took money from Sollazzo for losing a game to North Carolina State. When the team's star player, Sherman White, figured out what was going down, he also became part of the conspiracy. The Blackbirds had won 16 games that year, but a number of them were surprisingly close. Now everyone knew the reason why: the point spread was being con-trolled.

So great was the shock to Clair Bee when he learned of the bribes that some friends feared for his life. He lamented that his team "could have been a great one," and it took him a long time to get over the tre-mendous disappointment and to try to understand what had happened. The revelation all but destroyed the LIU basketball program for some seven years.

OPPOSITE TOP: *This bulletin board served as a grim reminder to players about keeping straight. It refers to a second scandal that occurred in early 1961. The Loyola players are co-captains John Crnokrak (left) and Jerry Verwey.*

OPPOSITE BOTTOM: *One of the scandal's biggest shockers was the admission by former Kentucky stars Dale Barnstable (left), Alex Groza (center) and Ralph Beard that they took a bribe to fix that Kentucky-Loyola NIT game in 1949. Beard and Groza were banned from the NBA for life.*

RIGHT: *Kentucky all-American Bill Spivey consults with his attorney, Elmer Drake, after being served a fugitive warrant in May of 1952. Spivey was charged only with perjury, but his potential pro career was gone.*

And there were more arrests. Another City College player, Floyd Layne, admitted taking $3000 to shave points in a pair of Garden games. And three of his teammates – Irwin Dambrot, Norm Mager and Herb Cohen – also admitted taking money. And when three more LIU players were charged, they admitted transgressions dating back to 1948. A pair of bookmakers, Eli Klukofsky and William Rivlin, were subsequently arrested for fixing games that year.

As the investigation continued authorities realized that most of the players had been too scared even to spend the money they had taken. The majority of them had just hidden it somewhere. And before long it also became apparent that the entire scandal should not be blamed entirely on New York and Madison Square Garden. Four of the five starters at Bradley, including All American Gene Melchiorre, were charged with taking bribes, and two of the games they were accused of fixing were at Bradley's field house, not the Garden.

Perhaps the biggest bombshell came when the Kentucky team was finally implicated. Remember the big NIT upset in 1949 when Loyola of Illinois upended the Wildcats in the first round of the NIT? It was an inexplicable turn of events when it happened, because the Kentucky team was so good that it had lost only a single game by a single point during the entire year. The team had then gone on to capture the NCAA title with relative ease after losing the Loyola game.

Now everyone understood. The Wildcats' two biggest stars, Alex Groza and Ralph Beard, along with Dale Barnstable, admitted having divided $2000 in return for shaving points in the Loyola game. The problem was that, in keeping the score close, the Wildcats had ended up blowing the game. That wasn't supposed to happen. And while the Kentucky players only admitted wrongdoing for that one game, the Lexington district attorney's office claimed that the majority of games the Wildcats played that year involved some kind of gambling.

By the time the scandal broke both Groza and Beard had established themselves as professional stars with the NBA's Indianapolis Olympians. They seemed well on their way to successful and lucrative pro careers, but once they were implicated, NBA Commissioner Maurice Podoloff acted swiftly and decisively, banning both players from the National Basketball Association for life. The two had paid a heavy price.

Unfortunately for Adolph Rupp the embarrassment wasn't over. He also learned that another of his former players, Jim Line, was also a go-between and had made offers of bribes to Walter Hirsch, as well as to the newest Kentucky star, Bill Spivey. Hirsch was convicted on a charge of fixing games, and while Spivey was only indicated on charges

of perjury, that was enough for Podoloff to ban him from ever entering the NBA.

Before the investigation ended it was also learned that some schools were changing records and altering transcripts of ballplayers, helping some to be admitted and then keeping them eligible for basketball any way they could. The whole system, it seemed, needed an overhaul.

Some of the fixers, such as Salvatore Sollazzo, received heavy sentences. A number of players, like White, Warner and Roth, got minor prison terms ranging from six months to a year. Others received suspended sentences, but all would have a difficult time putting their lives back on track. Their names would be remembered as part of college basketball's first, and worst, point shaving and fixing scandal. There would be others from time to time, but the first one, like baseball's Black Sox Scandal, would always carry the greatest stigma.

One of the most telling and prophetic statements regarding the entire scandal came from Judge Paul S. Streit of the court of general sessions. Judge Streit heard a good deal of the case and in summing up his feelings said:

The responsibility for the sports scandal must be shared not only by the crooked fixers and corrupt players, but also by the college administrations, coaches and alumni groups who participated in this evil system of commercialism and overemphasis . . . I found, among other vices, that the sport was commercialized and professionalized; devices, frauds and probable fraud were employed to matriculate unqualified students to college; flagrant violations of amateur rules by colleges, coaches and players; and illegal scouting, recruiting and subsidization of players.

The question was, would it happen again? The conditions would always be there. All it would take would be some human weakness, a touch of greed and maybe some naivete, for there would always be predators waiting to take advantage of susceptible situations and people. The answer, alas, is obvious: point shaving and fixing has occurred since and may, for all we know, be going on right now. But any athlete who is approached, or is thinking of becoming involved in some sort of scam, perhaps should heed the words of one player whose life was put on hold by the scandal of the 1950s.

"Tell any others who are tempted to do what I did to look at me," the player said. "I'm a fine example. I did it because I wanted to be grown up. Sounds funny, doesn't it? I mean I was sick and tired of asking my father for money all the time."

The Game Comes Back

The 1950-51 season hardly ended on a high note. The rancid smell of scandal was still in the air, and every game that didn't turn out the way it was supposed to inevitably raised some questions. The NCAA tried to enhance its tournament by expanding to 16 teams, but that didn't help dissipate the cloud that still hung heavy over the entire sport.

Despite being devastated by the revelations that his greatest team had been involved in the scandal, Adolph Rupp again put together a competitive team at Kentucky. He had three top youngsters, Cliff Hagan, Frank Ramsey and Lou Tsioropoulos to join with big Bill Spivey, giving the Wildcats another strong team. They would go on to win the NCAA title by topping Kansas State 68-58 in the final game. (Shortly afterward, Spivey's college career would end when he was indicated for perjury in the scandals.) The contest was played in Minneapolis, as the NCAA, also reeling from the results of the probe, decided to get as far away from Madison Square Garden as possible.

In the NIT Brigham Young defeated Dayton 62-43 to win the title, although both crowns that year did not have the same prestige as in prior seasons. There seemed to be an emptiness about the entire season and post-season. The question was: how long would it last?

Fortunately for the game of basketball, the sport was just entering the era where the modern player was about to emerge. The day of the set shot was slowly coming to an end. The next decade would bring about a proliferation of outstanding big men and several obvious superstars. The guards and forwards would be bigger and faster and would begin shooting jump shots from all over the court. It would be the charisma of the players who emerged in the years following the scandal that would really bring the game back.

The list of All American players who entered the college ranks during the decade of the 1950s reads like a Who's Who of both college and professional basketball, since they are remembered today as pioneers – creative, innovative players who helped change the face of the game and bring it into the modern age. Many of them are today members of the Basketball Hall of Fame. Included in this list are Clyde Lovellette, Dick Groat, Cliff Hagan, Rod Hundley, Bob Pettit, Frank Selvy, Sihugo Green, Bill Russell, Tom Heinsohn, Wilt Chamberlain, Guy Rodgers, Elgin Baylor, Oscar Robertson, Jerry West and Jerry Lucas. And that's only a short list of the top players. There were many, many others just a notch below who nevertheless excited fans

OPPOSITE: *Adolph Rupp had his Wildcats back on top in 1951. The team featured future pro stars Frank Ramsey (30) and Cliff Hagan (seated next to Rupp), but Bill Spivey (77) never made it as a result of the scandals.*

ABOVE: *Little Johnny O'Brien of Seattle was one of the new players who helped fans forget about the scandals in 1952.*

LEFT: *Duke's Dick Groat was a future baseball star.*

all over the country and made their own contribution to the sport in the wake of the scandals.

Though the court game has always been dominated by the big man, it was a number of ultra-talented guards who made the news in the immediate post-scandal period. The first of these was Dick Groat, a six-footer from Duke who led the nation in scoring during the 1950-51 season. Groat would go on to set a three-year national scoring mark, and, yes, he was the same Dick Groat who would later become a top shortstop for the Pirates and Cardinals, winning the National League's Most Valuable Player Award in 1960.

A year later, in 1951-52, a pair of 5ft 9in twins began thrilling fans with their exploits at Seattle University. Johnny and Eddie O'Brien were double-trouble for opponents who tried to keep up with these speedy backcourt men. During that year Johnny O'Brien became the first college player to go over the 1000-point mark for a single season. Also that year he played center in an exhibition game against the Harlem Globetrotters. All O'Brien did in that one was score 43 points, putting on a show that had master Globetrotter showman Goose Tatum marveling at his skills. "That Johnny O.," Tatum said, "He's not a little man; he's a big man!"

Then, in the 1951-52 playoffs, a big man took over. He was 6ft 9in, 270-pound Clyde Lovellette of the University of Kansas. Big Clyde played an inside power game not seen since the days of George Mikan, but he could also go outside and pop the one-hander, as he would later often do during his days in the pros. Lovellette and his Kansas teammates had some help from St. John's in the NCAA tourney that year.

ABOVE: *The game was on its way back in 1953. Here, Indiana's Don Schlundt goes inside for two points during the Hoosiers' 69-68 NCAA title victory over Kansas. Schlundt scored 30 points in the narrow victory.*

RIGHT: *The 1952 Kansas team featured burly center Clyde Lovellette (center). The Jayhawks took the national title for "Phog" Allen that year by beating St. John's 80-63. Lovellette scored 33 points and grabbed 17 rebounds.*

The Redmen knocked off top-ranked Kentucky 64-57, then took the measure of second-seeded Illinois and their star center, John "Red" Kerr, 61-59. And when the unheralded Redmen reached the finals, Kansas was waiting for them.

The Jayhawks had beaten TCU, with Lovellette scoring 31, and then had topped St. Louis, the burly center setting an NCAA tourney mark with 44 points. In the finals Lovellette made it look easy. He dominated the Redmen inside, scoring 33 points and grabbing 17 rebounds, and Kansas gave its veteran coach, Phog Allen, his first NCAA title, 80-63. Lovellette's final two points also gave him a new record of 1888 for the season, enabling him to pass the 1886 mark set by Dick Groat just a few days earlier.

There was also some excitement in the NIT that year. The fans hadn't deserted the Garden or the tournament, despite the still linger-

ing spectre of scandal, and nearly 19,000 of them jammed the arena to see the final game between LaSalle of Philadelphia and Dayton. In that game, LaSalle's exciting 6ft 6in freshman, Tom Gola, scored 22 points as the Explorers won the title 75-64. He was yet another of the new generation of players who were bringing life and excitement back to the game.

Lovellette had averaged 28.4 points a game for the season, while Groat banged away at a 26.0 clip. The Duke star also led the nation in assists. O'Brien had 1051 points for Seattle, and another young forward from LSU, freshman Bob Pettit, averaged 25.5 points a game.

The following year there was even more excitement. Johnny O'Brien kept pumping away at Seattle and set a career mark of 2537 points. Like Dick Groat, the O'Brien twins would forego professional basketball to become major league baseball players with the Pirates. But unlike Groat, neither would become a star, having relatively short careers before retiring.

But despite his high scoring, John O'Brien wasn't the top point-getter for the 1952-53 season. That honor went to 6ft 3in Frank Selvy of Furman, who scored at a 29.5 clip for the year, including a high game of 63 against Mercer. Indiana won the NCAA title with an exciting 69-68 victory over the Lovellette-less Kansas Jayhawks. Center Don Schlundt led Indiana with 30 points, while guard Bob Leonard had 12. In earlier rounds, Bob Houbregs of Washington had already broken Lovellette's year-old record by scoring 45 points against Seattle. Johnny O'Brien had scored 42 in his team's opener before they lost to Washington, and sophomore Bob Pettit had 28 and 29 in the two

OPPOSITE TOP: *Action from the 1952 NCAA title game as St. John's Ron MacGilvray scores a pair between three Kansas defenders.*

OPPOSITE BOTTOM: *A smiling Frank Selvy of Furman celebrates his breaking of Clyde Lovellette's three-year scoring record of 1888 points. Selvy would average 41.7 points a game in 1954, including an incredible 100 points in a game against Newberry College.*

RIGHT: *Award winners at the end of 1953 included, left to right, Seton Hall coach Honey Russell, his center Walter Dukes, LaSalle's great Tom Gola, and Holy Cross' electrifying Bob Cousy.*

BELOW: *Indiana's 1953 Big Ten champs pose for a team picture. The scandal over, basketball was beginning to grow once again.*

games LSU played before being eliminated. Great individual play seemed to be becoming the norm rather than the exception.

In the NIT, which was beginning to lose some of its luster to the NCAA, Seton Hall won the crown by beating St. John's 58-46 behind seven-footer Walter Dukes' 21 points.

In 1953-54 the individual achievements of the great new players continued to dazzle the basketball world. Fortunately, the fans kept coming to see the new stars perform. And in a year of great performances, perhaps the most unbelievable mark of all was set by Frank Selvy.

The Furman guard was the son of a Kentucky coal miner, and for awhile it looked as if he would follow the basketball tradition of his home state and join Adolph Rupp at Kentucky. But Selvy was a late bloomer who was just 5ft 4in as a high school freshman, and even though he had become a six-footer by the time he graduated, Rupp still felt he was too small to play for the Wildcats. So Selvy opted for Furman university in Greenville, South Carolina.

He got better each year, and by the time he was a senior in 1953-54 he was ready to set the college basketball world on end with his amazing scoring feats. For openers, he would average 41.7 points a game for the season, an unheard of total for those days. Selvy sometimes seemed unstoppable, and never more so than on the night of February 13, 1954. Furman was playing Newberry College in the first-ever basketball game to be televised in South Carolina. And with his parents, friends and neighbors all in attendance, Frank Selvy did something that is talked about to this very day.

ABOVE: *Tom Heinsohn followed Bob Cousy as a star at Holy Cross, and later followed Cooz to the Boston Celtics.*

ABOVE RIGHT: *Tom Gola was a star at LaSalle right from his freshman year of 1951-52.*

OPPOSITE: *A whole new era was born when center Bill Russell began playing for the University of San Francisco. In this January 1956 game against San Jose State, Russell (6) leads the Dons of San Francisco to their 41st straight victory.*

There was a hint in the air when Selvy scored 24 points in the first quarter of action. But how often has a player been red hot for a quarter or half, only to cool down? And, indeed, Selvy seemed to cool when he added "just" 13 more in the next 10 minutes, to finish the half with 37. But then he began to tune up again in the next 10 minutes, and pretty soon his teammates were feeding him the ball whenever they could. By the time the final 10 minutes began Selvy had 62 points, and everyone knew they were seeing something very special. The only question now was how high could he go?

Furman had the game in hand, and they were letting Newberry shoot quickly so they could get the ball back and give it to Selvy. Their star continued to hit shots from everywhere. He sailed past Bill Milkvy's single-game scoring of 73 points and then went for more. With only 35 seconds remaining in the game Frank Selvy was at the 90-point mark, itself an utterly amazing accomplishment. But he still wasn't finished.

Using the clock to their advantage the Furman team continued to work to their star, and Selvy responded. In the next 30 seconds he scored eight more points. Now, with the clock ticking off those final seconds, he had the ball again. Newberry had two players on him, and all that was left was a last-second heave from just inside the half court line. And it went in! Frank Selvy had done what most people felt was impossible: he had scored 100 points in a single basketball game. His performance, to this day, remains one of the greatest in the history of the college game.

Selvy wasn't the only great hoop star of that 1953-54 season.

ABOVE: *San Francisco coach Phil Woolpert shouts instructions to the floor during a close game. Woolpert's tactics revolved around defense, for which both Russell and K. C. Jones were ideally suited.*

OPPOSITE: *Guard K. C. Jones was a perfect compliment to center Russell with the Dons. Both players were genuinely outstanding, and both would later work their magic with the Boston Celtics.*

The early favorite for the NCAA title that year was once again the Kentucky Wildcats. Adolph Rupp's latest superteam sailed through their regular 25-game slate without a loss. But just before the NCAA championship was set to begin the Wildcats ran into some tough luck. Rupp's three stars – Cliff Hagan, Frank Ramsey and Lou Tsiropoulas – were all declared ineligible because they had earned enough credits for graduation. That put the Wildcats out of action and opened the tournament to the rest of the field.

With the field wide open it was Tom Gola who stepped to the fore. In LaSalle's opening game against Fordham the Explorers needed a late comeback to tie and overtime to win 76-74, with Gola getting 28. Then, in an 88-81 win over North Carolina State, the LaSalle star garnered 26 points and 26 rebounds. Next came Navy and a 64-48 LaSalle win, with Gola scoring 22 points and taking down 24 boards. In the semifinals against Penn State Gola had to settle for 19 points, but his club won easily, 69-54. LaSalle was now in the finals.

The Bradley Braves, no strangers to NCAA playoffs, would be LaSalle's opponent by virtue of their 74-72 win over Southern California. And LaSalle quickly found that the Braves would not be an easy foe. The first half was nip and tuck, as Bradley came away with a one-point lead of 43-42. At halftime, Coach Loeffler decided to make a strategy change. He switched from a man-to-man defense into a zone, and that made all the difference. The Explorers took charge and went on to win the game and the championship 92-76. Gola had 19 more points in this one and earned the MVP prize hands down.

With 24 teams for the first time, the NCAA tourney was bigger and better than ever. But the NIT was exciting as well, as Tom Heinsohn and Togo Palazzi led Holy Cross to a 71-62 title win over Duquesne. Gola, Selvy, Cliff Hagan, Don Schlundt and Bob Pettit were first-team All Americans, but there were plenty of other fine players that year. Some of them were Larry Costello of Niagara, Bob Leonard of Indiana, Johnny Kerr of Illinois, Gene Shue of Maryland, Dick Ricketts and Sihugo Green of Duquesne and Maurice Stokes of St. Francis of Loretto, Pennsylvania.

With players like Selvy and Gola putting on great individual performances and helping their teams to win, college basketball seemed to finally be working its way out from under the shadow of scandal that had been plaguing it for the past several seasons. The game seemed to be gaining a new kind of maturity, especially with the number of great players proliferating each year and different schools taking turns producing top teams. So when the 1954-55 season began many fans were eagerly anticipating what this season would produce that was new and different.

It didn't take them long to find out. They were about to be introduced to a player who would revolutionize first the college game and later professional basketball with his spectacular style of play. His name was Bill Russell, and he was the 6ft 9in center for the University of San Francisco. No, Russell didn't have all the individual skills honed to a perfect pitch. In fact, he was far from a great shooter, and he wasn't really a super ballhandler. But he did something else so well that it enabled his team to control just about every game in which it played.

Bill Russell's game, you see, was defense. He worked hard at it, playing with an unyielding intensity for the full 40 minutes of every game. And once he put his game together he became by far college basketball's best shot blocker and rebounder. He was easily the most intimidating presence in the sport, and many a shooter would pull up, hesitate or change the trajectory of a shot because he knew he had to get around or over Bill Russell. But more often than not the big guy would still swoop down and swat the shot away.

To make matters worse for opponents Russell and his San Francisco teammates played for a defense-minded coach, Phil Woolpert, who knew just how to best harness his center's immense talents. Add to this mixture a 6ft 1in All American-caliber guard named K. C. Jones, plus a number of solid role players, and the team was ready to take off. Russell was a junior in 1954-55, and since the Dons had had a rather ordinary record of 14-7 the year before, they were ready to take a lot of people by surprise.

San Francisco opened the season with a pair of victories, then lost a 47-40 game to UCLA. No one knew it at the time, but it would be the

Another who was making news was LaSalle's Tom Gola. As a freshman two years earlier he had led his team to an NIT title. Older and better now, he and his Explorer teammates had set their sights on an NCAA title.

Gola was a perfect example of a hard-working player who had virtually taught himself the complete game. At 6ft 6in he often played center, and in two separate years he led the entire nation in rebounding, yet he wasn't a leaper. Even more amazingly, to this day he still holds the NCAA record for total career rebounds, with 2201. As his coach, Ken Loeffler, said "I've never seen any one player control a game by himself the way Gola does."

Years later Gola credited Loeffler and the type of game he taught for helping him become that complete player, the kind who was able to make the transition from a college center to a guard in the NBA.

"At LaSalle we played a five-man weave," he said. "Anybody could bring the ball up and we all had places to go on the court. We had nobody sitting in the pivot and the middle was always open to drives if you got by your man. So that's how I learned how to handle the basketball, how to shoot from the outside and eventually how to play guard for ten years in the NBA."

ABOVE: *Following on the heels of the 6ft-10in Bill Russell, the 7ft-1in Wilt Chamberlain came to Kansas University in 1956. He soon appeared to be a nearly unstoppable force in basketball.*

RIGHT AND OPPOSITE: *Wilt showcased his stuff in an intra-squad game as a freshman in February of 1956. This sequence shows him grabbing a rebound and turning around for an easy dunk.*

win over Dayton. But it was becoming more obvious than ever that the NCAA was *the* tournament, the one that would decide the national champion. It certainly had in 1955 and 1956.

The next season Bill Russell was gone, first off to help the United States win a gold medal in the 1956 Olympics, then to professional glory with the Boston Celtics. And while the college game would miss him, there would be plenty more upon which fans could focus in 1956-57.

One major announcement was the retirement of Forrest "Phog" Allen as the coach at Kansas after 46 years and 771 victories. Allen cer-

tainly left a legacy to his school and had been one of the last surviving links to the earliest days of the game, since he had succeeded the game's inventor, James Naismith, as the Jayhawks' coach. But he also left behind the seeds of his final triumph, and that was the battle to bring 7ft 1in center Wilt Chamberlain to Kansas.

Chamberlain, who had come out of Overbrook High School in Philadelphia, was a player who was as strong as he was tall and as dominant as any high school player ever. He was the object of a nationwide recruiting battle that was won by the retiring Phog Allen. So big Wilt took his wares to Kansas, and in 1956-57 he was in his sophomore year and

his first year of varsity competition.

There were already some who felt that Wilt Chamberlain was so good that his team would be virtually unstoppable. Wilt may have not had the all-consuming intensity of Bill Russell, but he was bigger and stronger, could rebound and block shots and was more rounded offensively. The Jayhawks, as expected, swept through their schedule, though there were a pair of blemishes. Two defeats, both to teams using deliberate stalling tactics, kept the Jayhawks from a perfect record in the regular season.

When Kansas entered the NCAA tournament that year they were by no means the clear-cut favorites. That's because there was a major unbeaten team that season, the University of North Carolina. The Tarheels had won 27 straight games under Coach Frank McGuire, and while they didn't have any single dominating player such as Chamberlain they were nevertheless a well balanced, well coached, deep team. When Kansas topped San Francisco 80-56, and North Carolina defeated Michigan State 74-70, the two teams prepared to meet for the NCAA title.

It was to be one of the most memorable games in NCAA history. North Carolina was led by sweet-shooting Lenny Rosenbluth, a 6ft 6in forward. But Coach McGuire had other fine players such as Joe Quigg, Pete Brennan and Tommy Kearns. And with all the Tar Heels hitting their shots early, North Carolina jumped out to a 19-7 lead. Kansas rallied behind Chamberlain, but at the half Carolina still led by seven at 29-22.

The two ballclubs continued to play their contrasting games in the second half. At one point Chamberlain began doing damage underneath, and the Jayhawks forged into the lead, three up on Carolina, with almost ten minutes left. Then first-year Kansas coach Dick Harp surprised everyone by going into a slowdown game. Kansas seemed to get a break when Rosenbluth fouled out with 1:45 left, having scored 20 points. Yet a shot by the Tarheels' Bob Young tied the low-scoring game at 46 at the end of regulation time.

Both clubs were cautious during the overtime period, not wanting to make a big mistake. The result was just a single hoop for each, and at the end of the first five-minute OT session it was still tied at 48-48. The second overtime was even more agonizing, in that neither team could score a single point. Now the two teams squared off once more for the third overtime period, the first triple overtime game in the NCAA final. This time Carolina came out fast, scoring four points and taking a 52-48 lead. But Kansas bounced back again, tying the game at 52, then taking a 53-52 lead with just 31 seconds remaining.

ABOVE: *In the 1957 NCAA final, Wilt finds himself hounded by North Carolina's Lenny Rosenbluth.*

RIGHT: *The Tar Heels celebrate after their triple overtime 54-53 NCAA victory over Kansas to complete an unbeaten season.*

OPPOSITE: *Seattle's Elgin Baylor was a 6ft-5in forward who could do everything on the court.*

The Tar Heels looked for the winning basket, but all they could get was a foul call as Joe Quigg tried to put in a rebound. Quigg then stepped calmly to the line and sank both free throws to give his club the lead. Seconds later he slapped away a Kansas inbounds pass, and the game was history. North Carolina had won 54-53, completing a 32-0 season and doing what some thought was impossible, defeating Wilt Chamberlain and his teammates.

That was the beginning of a strange period for Wilt. Despite his team's loss, he was the tourney MVP, and he returned the following year to lead his team again. Now almost every defense Kansas encountered was designed to stop the big guy. Teams played stalls and slowdowns; they double- and triple-teamed him; they harassed him, often pushing and shoving him, with lesser players acting as hatchetmen. Kansas slipped to 18-5 and didn't even win its own conference title.

When he looked around at what was happening Chamberlain began to take stock. He wasn't enjoying the kind of game being played to counter his size and skills, and he didn't think he would progress as a player by continuing at Kansas. So after the 1957-58 season he surprised everyone by announcing that he was leaving the Jayhawks to join the Harlem Globetrotters. A year later, when he was eligible, he went on to the NBA, where he would be an impact player and have

some memorable confrontations with Bill Russell. But as good as he was, Wilt's college career had been less than satisfying, much less than it could have been.

Russell and Chamberlain, however, were just the first of a whole new group of impact players who would be passing through the college ranks in the next several years. For instance, there was a 6ft 5in forward at Seattle University named Elgin Baylor who could do most of the things that both smaller and bigger men could do. He could take the ball and dribble end to end, finishing his journey with a series of "moves" that could fake even the quickest of defenders. At the same time he could go under the hoop and rebound with players six and seven inches taller. Baylor also seemingly had the ability to hang in the air longer than an opponent, making it look as if he was defying the laws of gravity.

In 1958 Baylor brought his Seattle team all the way to the NCAA finals, only to have their run stopped there by another of Adolph Rupp's balanced Kentucky teams. The score was 84-72, and The Baron had his fourth NCAA title. Baylor scored 25 points and pulled down 19 rebounds in his final college game. He, too, would go on to a brilliant pro career.

It was almost like a revolving door now, the way the great players came and went. Russell left the college ranks in 1956, Chamberlain and

Baylor in 1958, yet the game could quickly turn to others. For instance, a pair of incredible sophomores burst on to the college scene in 1958, and they would quickly add their own particular styles of brilliance to the sport. They were both guards, and their names were Oscar Robertson of the University of Cincinnati and Jerry West of West Virginia University.

The Big O, as Robertson was called, was a 6ft 5in guard of such superb talents that there are still people who call him the greatest all-around player ever. Robertson never seemed to need a period of adjustment. He was a superstar from the first game he played in college, and he was a superstar from the first game he played as a pro. As a sophomore at Cincinnati in 1957-58 he led the nation in scoring, with a 35.1 average. He would go on to be a three-time All America, and he remains the fourth all-time leading scorer in college basketball annals, with 2973 points. The respect for the Big O is universal. Many players and sportswriters have tried to describe his unique personal style and the qualities that made him so great. But perhaps it was Wilt Chamberlain who summed it up best when he said, "Oscar is not as fast as some ballplayers and not as good a shooter as others, but he knows how to put everything together better than anyone else."

Jerry West, who is often mentioned in the same breath with Robertson, was more of a pure guard at 6ft 3in. He didn't come on the scene as rapidly as the Big O, but once he got it together in 1959 he was a genuine All American and one of basketball's great clutch players. He loved it when the game was on the line, and more often than not he came through. He would later show the same characteristics with the Los Angeles Lakers of the NBA.

OPPOSITE ABOVE: *There are still some who call Oscar Robertson the greatest ever. The Big O came to Cincinnati in 1958 and began rewriting the book.*

OPPOSITE LEFT: *Sometimes it seemed as if West Virginia's Jerry West was a one-man gang.*

RIGHT: *An all-American at West Virginia and an all-Pro in the NBA, Jerry West was one of the great clutch players.*

The 1958-59 season saw both Cincinnati and West Virginia make it to the Final Four of the NCAA championships. But the Bearcats couldn't get past California in the semifinals. The Bears were a defense-minded club with a good 6ft 10 center in Darrall Imhoff, and they prevailed 64-58. West Virginia fared better because of Jerry West. In a second-round game against St. Joseph's, for instance, the Mountaineers trailed 67-49, with just 13 minutes left. Yet West wouldn't quit, and he rallied his club by scoring 21 points in just nine minutes. When it ended West Virginia had a 95-92 victory, and Jerry West had scored 36 points. Two more victories, including a semifinal win over Louisville, put West Virginia in the finals.

West again did his stuff in the final, only this time it wasn't quite enough. California's overall balance gave the Bears a 12-point lead early in the second half. Despite West's clutch shooting, his club fell a point short, losing the championship 71-70. West had scored 28 points and grabbed 11 rebounds, both game highs, but the star guard would have gladly traded in all his stats, his 160 points and MVP prize for one national championship.

So now the sport was on the brink of a new decade as the 1959-60 season began. The 1950s had been a decade of highs and lows, the low obviously being the scandals of 1950-51. The highs were the overall growth of the sport and the many great players who had appeared on

LEFT: *The turn of the decade was producing more and more great players. Jerry Lucas of Ohio State was a 6ft-8in center with exquisite timing and a real knowledge of how to play the game.*

OPPOSITE: *Lucas had the help to make Ohio State a great team. Forward John Havlicek was an all-American in his own right and went on to become an all-time great with the Boston Celtics.*

RIGHT: *The California Golden Bears upset West Virginia for the 1959 NCAA crown. A defense-minded team, the Bears were led by brilliant center Darrall Imhoff (40).*

the scene, convincing fans all over again of the greatness of the game. And perhaps no season captured the brilliant talents that were in college basketball as well as 1959-60. Robertson and West were back for their senior years, as was Darrall Imhoff. But there was more . . . much more.

In the Midwest there was a player and a team that would quickly capture the attention of the nation's hoop fans. The player was Jerry Lucas, a 6ft 8in, 230-pound center, and the school was Ohio State. Lucas would team with such other fine players as John Havlicek, Larry Siegfreid and Mel Nowell to form the heart of the Buckeye teams that would reach the NCAA finals for three consecutive years. And while the latter three were all fine players in their own right, it was Lucas around whom the team revolved.

Lucas had been an incredible high school player who had broken a

host of records, including the all-time scoring mark set by Wilt Chamberlain when he was at Overbrook High. The recruiting war to land this superstar player had raged furiously, and Lucas had received nearly 150 offers of scholarships, in all shapes and sizes. Some of the offers even contained promises of a job for his father. But to all these packages Jerry Lucas said no. Instead, he accepted an academic scholarship at Ohio State. For in addition to being a great basketball player Lucas was also a straight-A student.

On the court he used his brains as well as his body, and he played the game as it was supposed to be played, for Lucas always made sure he meshed his talent with the team surrounding him. He was completely unselfish, and he loved to pass and rebound as well as score. There were bigger, taller, stronger centers, but he could out-rebound nearly all of them because of his sense of positioning, his anticipation and his

OPPOSITE: *1960 was Ohio State's year. In a regional game against Western Kentucky, Jerry Lucas (11) was the dominant player on the floor.*

RIGHT: *Coach Fred Taylor and his 1960 Ohio State Buckeyes. Left to right: Taylor, Havlicek, Richie Hoyt, Bob Knight, Mel Nowell, Larry Siegfried and Lucas.*

BOTTOM: *The 1960 United States Olympic basketball team was one of the most powerful teams ever assembled. Just check the names in the photo.*

near-perfect timing. When Coach Fred Taylor surrounded Lucas with talented supporting players the team became a great one.

All these factors combined to make the final season of the decade outstanding. Robertson and West wanted one more shot at that elusive national championship, and all the other great players were trying to lead their teams to the Final Four.

At the end of the regular season it looked as if the Big O and his Bearcats teammates might finally make it. Cincinnati was 26-1 for the year and the top-ranked team in the Associated Press poll. They were an early favorite for the NCAA title, and when they whipped De Paul and Kansas behind the inspired play of Robertson in the Midwest regionals, they had reached the semifinals. Joining the Bearcats were New York University from the East, defending champion California from the West and Lucas and Ohio State from the Mideast.

1960 U.S. OLYMPIC BASKETBALL TEAM

Imhoff · Lucas · Bellamy · Holderson · Boozer · Dischinger · Robertson

Lane · A. Kelly · Smith · Arnette · West · Dean Nesmith Trainer

Warren Womble · Dutch Lonborg · Pete Newell

RIGHT: *Cincinnati upset Ohio State to take the 1961 crown with outstanding play from Tom Thacker (25) and Paul Hogue (22). The Bearcats won, 70-65, despite a 27-point, 12-rebound performance by Jerry Lucas.*

The Buckeyes had a pretty easy game in the semis, defeating NYU 76-54 because the Violets' 6ft 6in center, Tom "Satch" Sanders, just couldn't handle Lucas. Then, in a mild surprise, California rode the inside play of Imhoff to a 77-69 win over Cincinnati, sending Robertson and teammates to a tough defeat. The final game was almost anticlimactic. With all five Ohio State starters scoring in double figures, the Buckeyes rolled to a 37-19 first-half lead and an easy 75-55 victory, taking the title. Lucas led the way, with 16 points and 10 rebounds.

Following the season the United States had to pick an Olympic basketball team to represent the country at the Rome Olympics. The US ballclub would win the gold medal in a walk. And why not? On that Olympic team were Oscar Robertson, Jerry West, Jerry Lucas, Darrall Imhoff, Mel Nowell, 7ft 11in Walt Bellamy of Indiana, 6ft 7in Terry Dischinger of Purdue and several others. It may have been the greatest Olympic basketball team ever assembled, a team that could have entered the NBA as a group and been an instant winner and probable championship contender.

The decade of the 1960s started in a surprising manner. Nearly everyone expected Ohio State to continue as basketball's dominant team for another two years. In fact, many felt the Buckeyes would become the first team to win three straight NCAA tournaments. Beginning with Lucas, they certainly seemed to have the talent to do it. And, indeed, they would reach the final round as expected for the next two years. But they didn't win it. Each time they lost to the same

team, a team that had lost the greatest player in its history just a year before reaching the finals.

That team was the University of Cincinnati. The Bearcats never made the NCAA finals when the great Oscar Robertson was there, but Coach Ed Jucker had subsequently put together a more balanced ballclub, many of the players coming to Cincy because of the Big O. Center Paul Hogue, guards Tony Yates and Ton Thacker and forwards Bob Wiesenhahn and Ron Bonham aren't exactly household names, and none of them really made the transition to the pros, as did Lucas, Havlicek and Siegfried of Ohio State. Yet in head-to-head meetings for the NCAA title in both 1961 and 1962 the Bearcats came out on top.

The first game was a close one. Ohio State was ranked number one in both polls and was a heavy favorite to defeat the Bearcats, who had struggled in several earlier games. But in the final at Kansas City, Cincinnati would not let Ohio State take charge. The game was nip and tuck all the way, and with just a minute left Cincinnati held a two-point lead at 61-59. But then the Buckeyes' Bobby Knight (the same Bobby Knight who would make his name as a head coach at Indiana) drove in for a layup to tie the game. When neither club could score in the closing seconds the game went into overtime.

In the overtime the Bearcats surprised everyone by scrapping and clawing to a 70-65 victory. Lucas had 27 points and 12 rebounds in a losing cause, and he was named the tourney's Most Valuable Player. But the disappointment of losing was acute, and the Buckeyes im-

ABOVE: *Cincinnati repeated its triumph over Ohio State in the 1962 final, this time winning 71-59. Center Paul Hogue (with ball) had 22 points and 19 rebounds to pace the Bearcat attack.*

RIGHT: *Bearcat Coach Ed Jucker is hoisted up in victory after his ballclub took its second straight NCAA crown in 1962. It's a ride no coach ever forgets.*

ABOVE: *A dramatic 60-58 overtime victory made Loyola of Chicago the surprise winners of the 1963 title over Cincinnati.*

RIGHT: *Loyola's John Egan (11)*

OPPOSITE: *Rambler Vic Rouse (40).*

mediately began planning for the next season. Sure enough, by the start of the new season Ohio State was again the dominant team, number one in both polls.

There was a brief setback in 1961 when another point-shaving scandal was uncovered. It wasn't nearly as widespread as the first one, and people were better prepared for the possibility of this happening. After all, there were now so many teams and so many players that it was all but impossible to police the entire sport. Though it was a sad thing to have to admit, most people accepted that point shaving would be a reality that would have to be dealt with every now and then.

In the meantime Ohio State and Cincinnati were again the two teams making it to the NCAA finals. The Buckeyes topped Wake Forest 84-68 but lost Lucas to an injury in the process. Cincinnati beat a new entry in the Final Four sweepstakes, John Wooden's UCLA Bruins. It wasn't easy, but the Bearcats prevailed 72-70 when center Paul Hogue put together a game of 36 points and 19 rebounds. But the young UCLA team would be back. And with a vengeance.

The final was almost anti-climactic. Lucas played, despite his injury, but wasn't his usual self, and Paul Hogue put together a great game, with 22 points and 19 more rebounds, to lead the Bearcats to a 71-59 win and a second straight national championship.

A year later the Bearcats attempted to become the first team to win three straight titles, and this time they were favored to do it. Lucas and Havlicek had graduated to the pros, so Ohio State wasn't a factor.

LEFT: *Big Walt Bellamy cradles the ball for the University All-Stars as he's surrounded by a trio of Peoria Cats during Olympics trial basketball in April 1960.*

BELOW: *Bradley's Chet "The Jet" Walker goes up for two of his school-record 50 points as the Braves beat the California Aggies 102-65 in December of 1960. Walker was still another of the new crop of college players who went on to star in the pros.*

OPPOSITE: *Center Nate Thurmond of Bowling Green grabs a rebound in 1963 action against Notre Dame. Thurmond was also a great rebounder in the NBA.*

Cincy marched into the Final Four, then defeated Oregon State easily, 80-46, so now the Bearcats were in a position to make it three. They would be meeting a surprising Cinderella team in the finals. Loyola of Chicago under Coach George Ireland were the surprise of the tourney. And the Ramblers were solid: the team featured a genuine All American in guard Jerry Harkness and some of very fine players such as Vic Rouse, Les Hunter and John Egan.

The Ramblers showed they were for real in the semifinals when they surprised second-ranked Duke, a team that featured All Americans Art Heyman and Jeff Mullins. Yet, despite their presence, it was the Ramblers who rolled, winning the game easily, 94-75, to reach the finals. This time it was a barnburner. Cincy led early and midway through the second period had a seemingly comfortable 45-30 lead.

Then the Ramblers came back. They kept closing the gap, and, with just seconds left, Cincinnati led 53-52. But Cincy's Larry Shingleton made only the front end of a one-and-one, and Harkness got the rebound, drove the length of the floor and made the tying hoop just before the buzzer. So it was overtime again, and once more it was back and forth until the final seconds, when Loyola's Rouse became the hero by rebounding a missed shot and putting it back up for the win. The Cincinnati reign was over, 60-58.

Despite the Cincinnati-Ohio State dominance of the past several years, there had been many outstanding players all over the college basketball scene. Among them were Tom Stith of St. Bonaventure, Terry Dischinger of Purdue, Chet Walker of Bradley, Walt Bellamy of Indiana, Billy McGill of Utah, Len Chappell of Wake Forest, Heyman and Mullins of Duke, Barry Kramer of NYU, Rod Thorn of West Virginia and Nate Thurmond of Bowling Green. And this merely prefigured the shape of things to come, for players of such caliber would keep on coming and coming.

PART IV

Basketball, Supersport

The players would get bigger, stronger and faster as the years passed. Larry Bird (33) and Earvin "Magic" Johnson (with ball) wouldn't emerge until the late 1970s. But both of them were new breed complete players.

Bruin Dynasty

When the 1963-64 season began most eyes were on individual players. The Ohio State-Cincinnati dominance had ended, since most of the star players on those teams had left school, and when the new year began there didn't seem to be any new superteam on the horizon. Indeed, there were now so many great players around that perhaps no one school *could* dominate, and the NCAA tournament would be up for grabs every year, with surprise teams like Loyola of Chicago becoming the norm rather than the exception. At least that was the thinking of many college basketball observers.

But such speculation proved, at the least, to be premature, for a team was about to emerge that would dominate college basketball in a way it hasn't been dominated before or since. Whenever one group of its players would graduate, another would be ready to take their places. And the team's wily coach always knew exactly how to handle his teams, whether he was working around a dominant superstar or just playing a balanced game with a group of talented athletes.

The coach was John Wooden and the school was UCLA. The Bruins had made some noise when they reached the NCAA semifinals in 1962, but as the 1963-64 season got underway Wooden had his team ready to move as never before. And once the Bruins reached the top they would be very unwilling to relinquish their crown. In fact, UCLA woulds capture an unprecedented ten NCAA championships in 12 years, including an incredible seven in a row.

LEFT: *UCLA's Coach John Wooden.*

ABOVE RIGHT: *Bill Bradley of Princeton, now a U.S. Senator, was one of the best in 1964-65.*

BELOW RIGHT: *Michigan's Cazzie Russell was another great all-American of 1964-65.*

Coach Wooden, who had been an All America player at Purdue from 1930-32, would become known as the Wizard of Westwood for his coaching exploits. But he would also have a succession of great players, including two of college basketball's most dominant centers ever, Lew Alcindor (later known as Kareem Abdul-Jabbar) and Bill Walton. But Wooden's true greatness would come from the fact that he won with them and without them during an era in which his teams had an almost uncanny ability to win, especially at NCAA tournament time.

At the outset of the 1963-64 season, however, the fans were still looking at individuals. One player who had a great deal of charisma then was Bill Bradley of Princeton, the same Bill Bradley who would become a United States Senator in the 1980s. Back in the 1960s he was a 6ft 5in guard-forward who would take unheralded Princeton to some surprising heights, while establishing himself as one of the really great college players.

As good as he was, Bill Bradley had company. There were burly Cazzie Russell of Michigan, Dave Stallworth of Wichita State, Cotton Nash of Kentucky and Jeff Mullins of Duke. But while all of these players lived up to expectations, it was UCLA that began attracting attention as the season wore on. The Bruins were simply playing great basketball.

RIGHT: *Cotton Nash (with ball) of Kentucky was still another of the many players from the early 1960s who electrified the ever-growing college basketball crowds with a great, all-round game.*

BELOW LEFT: *Three more all-Americans grace the court in this game between Duke and NYU. The Blue Devils' Jeff Mullins (44) and Art Heyman (25) were both standout performers, while NYU's Barry Kramer (55) brought New York crowds to its feet with his leaping wizardry.*

BELOW RIGHT: *Wichita State had its own all-American performer in Dave "The Rave" Stallworth.*

John Wooden always believed in a controlled, yet fastbreaking offense, plus a trapping, pressing defense that could disrupt almost any offense. Coaching in California near a pair of very defense-minded coaches – Phil Woolpert at San Francisco and Pete Newell at California – Wooden resisted the temptation to be influenced by their success and stuck by his system. Then, in the early 1960s, he finally began getting the ballplayers he wanted.

One of the first stars to appear at the Westwood campus was Walt Hazzard, a slick 6ft 2in guard from Philadelphia. The Bruins had a small but very quick team then, and Wooden needed a player to run the offense and defense. That was the year the ballclub made it to the semifinals. Then, a year later, in 1962-63, Hazzard was joined by another quick guard, 6ft 1in Gail Goodrich, and by a fine forward, Keith Erickson. By 1963-64 Wooden had an explosive sixth man in Kenny Washington. While he didn't have a starter over 6ft 5in that year, Wooden mapped out game plans to defeat taller, stronger teams. His players carried out his orders to perfection, and the Bruins started their roll.

In the opening game of the 1963-64 season the Bruins played a much taller Brigham Young quintet. Wooden ordered his team into their full-court press, and the Cougars didn't stand a chance. The Bruins won the game 113-71, showing the basketball world that they could no longer be overlooked. In fact, as the season progressed, the Bruins lost not a single game. During December, they easily outclassed Cazzie Russell's Michigan team, then rolled through the rest of their schedule to post a perfect 26-0 record for the season.

With everyone gunning for them, the Bruins had to work hard through the regional rounds of the NCAA tournament. They made it to the semifinals, where they rode a 28-point Keith Erickson performance to a 90-84 victory over Kansas State. Then, in the finals, they overcame a much taller Duke squad to win their first national title 98-83. Goodrich had 27 points in the final and Washington 26, while Hazzard was named the tournament's Most Valuable Player.

Wooden then set about proving that his victory wasn't a flash in the pan. Hazzard was now gone, but solid players like Edgar Lacey and Mike Lynn had joined the ballclub. After an opening 110-83 upset at the hands of Illinois the Bruins won 24 of their next 25 games and seemed more than ready to defend their championship. It would be an exciting Final Four, because it not only featured UCLA, but also Princeton and

OPPOSITE: *John Wooden's first championship teams at UCLA were led by a pair of slick guards, Walt Hazzard and Gail Goodrich (25), both of whom could drive around bigger, but slower, men.*

ABOVE: *Walt Hazzard in a great moment for any player: cutting down the net after his team had won the national championship. The Bruins had just defeated Duke 98-83 to begin their title run in 1964.*

RIGHT: *Not only was UCLA the champ in 1963-64, but the Bruins were unbeaten in 30 games. This unusual publicity photo celebrates the team's success.*

JACK HIRSCH
Forward

KEITH ERICKSON
Forward

FRED SLAUGHTER
Center

GAIL GOODRICH
Guard

UCLA BRUINS 1964
National Champions & No. 1 Team
Wins 30 ••• Losses 0

JOHN WOODEN
Head Coach

JERRY NORMAN
Asst. Coach

WALT HAZZARD
Guard

KIM STEWART
Forward-Center

KENNY WASHINGTON
Guard-Forward

VAUGHN HOFFMAN
Center

DENNIS MINISHIAN
Senior Manager

DOUG McINTOSH
Center-Forward

RICH LEVIN
Forward

MIKE HUGGINS
Guard

CHUCK DARROW
Guard

RIGHT: *Beginning in 1964, the word was knock off the Bruins. Not many teams could do it, but Iowa was one that gave it a try.*

BELOW: *When 7ft-1in center Lew Alcindor arrived in 1966-7, the Bruins were nearly unbeatable.*

Michigan, with Bill Bradley and Cazzie Russell, who were two of the more exciting stars of the year. They would be joined on the All America team by Goodrich, Rick Barry of Miami and Fred Hetzel of Davidson.

UCLA had little trouble with Wichita State in its semifinal, winning 108-89 behind 28 by Goodrich and 24 by Lacey. The other semi saw powerful Michigan take Princeton 93-76, despite 29 by Bradley. Then, in the finals, the Bruin running game proved too much for the slower Wolverines. With Goodrich exploding for 42 points UCLA made it two straight, winning 91-80. Russell showed his greatness with 28 in a losing cause. Big news was also made in the consolation game that year. Princeton topped Wichita State 118-82, as Bill Bradley set the tourney on fire with 58 points, good enough to earn the future Rhodes scholar, New York Knick and United States Senator the Most Valuable Player award.

If Wooden had wowed the basektball world with his two straight victories, he was now preparing to tower over it. In the fall of 1965 he went out and signed the most prized recruit in the country, 7ft 2in Lew Alcindor from New York's Power Memorial High School. It didn't take long for his coach to see what Alcindor could do. Leading the Bruin freshmen (freshmen could not play varsity then) against the varsity, Alcindor and his first-year teammates whipped their varsity counter-

parts handily, 75-60. The UCLA varsity was good, but not great that year, so the rest of the basketball world knew it had better scramble for the national title. For in the following season UCLA would have Alcindor, and that could tie things up for three more years.

Alcindor certainly came to California with impressive credentials. At 11 years of age he was already 6ft 4in, and when he began playing for Power Memorial he was 6ft 6in. But while he kept growing rapidly, he never went through a gawky, uncoordinated stage. His skills were always highly developed, and he led his high school team to a 95-6 record during his years there. In fact, five of the six losses came when he was a freshman. After that he led his club to an amazing 71 consecutive victories.

Besides his obvious talents Lew Alcindor had something else. He was a total team player who didn't worry about his individual stats or press clippings. He just wanted to win, and that's another reason he and John Wooden made an almost perfect marriage. Coach and player translated into team, and UCLA, perhaps more than any other top ball-club of the era, played a total team game with a team concept. The big guy was the final piece to the puzzle, the link that would make a good team great.

But with Alcindor still a year away, the 1965-66 season was looked at as wide open by most coaches, and as it came down to NCAA time everyone began calling the 1966 event the "Last-Chance Tournament." And, indeed, the Bruins *were* having a bit of a down year as they waited for their sensational freshman team to come of age.

By the end of the season there were some of the expected contenders and one unexpected entry. Adolph Rupp brought in another one of his fine Kentucky teams, and the Wildcats were ranked number one at the end of the regular season. It wasn't a big team. The leading scorers were guards Louie Dampier and Pat Riley (the same Pat Riley who became the highly-successful coach of the Los Angeles Lakers in the 1980s), and the team didn't have a starter over 6ft 5in. Someone dubbed them "Rupp's Runts," but they could play, and it wasn't a surprise when the ballclub made it to the Final Four.

Joining them were the number two-ranked team, Duke, featuring guard Bob Verga and forward Jack Marin, both All America candidates. The number three team that year was the surprise. They were the Miners of Texas Western (now called Texas El-Paso), and they

checked into the Final four with just a single loss for the entire season. Coach Don Haskins' team featured the likes of David Lattin, Bobby Joe Hill, Willie Worsley, Neville Shed, Willie Cager and Orsten Artis. None was a superplayer, but under Haskins they came together as a team and could score, rebound and play defense. Utah was the fourth team to reach the finals, but the Utes were not considered a threat.

In the semis Kentucky used its speed to squeak past Duke 83-79. Then Texas Western had to go against Utah. The Miners had been surviving close games to get there, like a 78-76 overtime win over Cincinnati and an 81-80 thriller against Kansas. Against Utah the Miners played a strong game and emerged as 85-78 winners. Now it would be their power against the speed of Kentucky. Coach Rupp was going for

ABOVE: *Texas Western won the 1966 NCAA title in a tourney dubbed the* "Last Chance," *because a year later Alcindor was at UCLA.*

OPPOSITE: *Other outstanding players: Gary Bradds (35) of Ohio* *State and Jack Marin (24) of Duke University.*

LEFT: *Action from the 1966 title game. Texas Western's Nevil Shed goes up for a rebound as Kentucky's Thad Jaracz and Pat Riley (right) watch.*

BELOW: *Bobby Joe Hill (14) of Texas Western drives past Kentucky's Tommy Kron (30) during NCAA title game action in 1966.*

his fifth national title, and for that reason The Baron and his team were sentimental favorites.

The final was a good, though not overly-exciting, ballgame. Texas Western just had a little too much height and power for Kentucky and even matched the Wildcats in the speed department. The Miners led the game all the way, though never blowing it open, and they won the title by a 72-65 score, as Hill led them with 20 points. Strangely enough, the tourney MVP was Utah's Jerry Chambers, who had 143 points in four games, though his club lost in the semis and again in the consolation. To some, Chambers' selection showed the weakness of the field. But not to worry, Alcindor and UCLA were on the way.

It didn't take long for the Bruins to serve notice in 1966-67. Wooden started a team of four sophomores and a junior, and in their first game they whipped Southern California 105-90. All Lew Alcindor did in that one was score a team record 56 points!

Joining Alcindor in the starting lineup were junior Mike Warren, a cat-quick, six-foot guard. With him in the backcourt was 6ft 3in sophomore Lucius Allen, another outstanding player. One forward was 6ft 7in Lynn Shackelford, a deadly shooter from the corner, and the other was Ken Heitz, who was just under 6ft 4in but was another tenacious defensive player. And the club had a bench, too.

To no one's surprise opponent after opponent fell to the Bruin jug-

65 2 72

LEFT: *Coach Don Haskins (2nd from left) and the rest of his Miners celebrate their 1966 victory. It would be the last non-UCLA victory until 1974.*

BELOW: *From his first varsity game with the Bruins, Lew Alcindor was a dominant force. The big guy sometimes seemed unstoppable, with his size, fluid movement and great shooting.*

gernaut. The only team coming close to upsetting Alcindor and company was Southern Cal, which had taken a pasting in the opener. This time the Trojans tried a stall and cut the score way down. UCLA had to scramble, but they won 40-35. When it was time for the NCAA tourney, the Bruins were unbeaten and overwhelming favorites. Alcindor had averaged more than 29 points a game for the regular season and had led the nation by hitting on a record 66.7 percent of his shots. In addition, Warren, Allen, and Shackelford had all averaged double figures, with the two guards playing at close to All American level.

So dominant were the Bruins that the NCAAs almost looked like practice games. First they topped Wyoming 109-60, then Pacific 80-64. In the Final Four they defeated the University of Houston and its All America forward, Elvin Hayes, 73-58. Then they won the title with an easy 79-64 victory over surprising Dayton. For John Wooden it was a third national title in four years. And, good news for everyone else, he had his entire team coming back the following year.

In 1967-68 there was a new rule, and some say it was made to neutralize Lew Alcindor: dunking was outlawed. Only it didn't really stop Alcindor, Hayes or any of the other multi-talented players in the game. All it did was take some excitement out of the sport, and several years later the rule was rescinded.

But it was still a great year. UCLA almost lost its opener to All American Rick Mount and Purdue. But a last-second jumper by reserve Bill Sweek won it 73-71. Then the Bruins rolled, as expected, running their winning streak to 47 games. Their next game was a big one against Houston, set for the giant Astrodome, with more than 50,000 fans expected. Alcindor had suffered a scratched eyeball eight days earlier and had been hospitalized, but with one practice under his belt he decided to play. Yet it was obvious right away that he wasn't 100 percent.

But Elvin Hayes was. The Big E, as he was called, put on one of the great shows in college hoop history. Hitting shot after shot from all over, Hayes had 29 points at the half, but his team had only a 46-43 lead. After intermission the big forward cooled a bit and UCLA tied it at 54. After that it was back and forth, with the game tied at 65, and again at 69. With less than 30 seconds remaining Hayes got the ball and drove toward the hoop. Whistle! He was fouled. The Big E then calmly sank both free throws, and the Cougars were able to hold on for a 71-69 victory. Hayes scored 39 points, while Alcindor, hampered by the eye

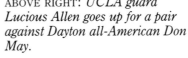

ABOVE LEFT: *UCLA's Mike Warren battles against North Carolina in 1968. Warren was another of the all-American-caliber players who complimented Alcindor during his Bruin days.*

ABOVE RIGHT: *UCLA guard Lucious Allen goes up for a pair against Dayton all-American Don May.*

LEFT: *UCLA Coach John Wooden, the fabled Wizard of Westwood, shouts orders from the bench.*

OPPOSITE: *Lew Alcindor goes high above the rim to block a shot by North Carolina star Charlie Scott (33) during the 1968 title game. The Bruins won easily, 78-55, with Alcindor scoring 34.*

injury, hit on only four of 18 shots from the floor and finished with 15.

It was to be the Bruins only loss of the year. And when they reached the Final Four at the Los Angeles Sports Arena they got their revenge. Meeting Houston in the semifinals, the Bruins won going away, 101-69, holding Hayes to just ten points, while Alcindor scored 19 and added 18 rebounds. The Bruins then crushed North Carolina in the final 78-55, with the big guy getting 34. It was yet another national title.

The loss of the starting backcourt of Allen and Warren in 1968-69 didn't seem to matter much to the Bruins. Alcindor and company were unbeaten until the final regular season game of the year. An upset at the hands of Southern Cal kept the Bruins from a perfect year, but in the tournament UCLA played as if they owned it. They swept into the finals as if it were old hat, then topped Purdue 92-72, for their third straight title and their fifth in six years.

In his final game as a Bruin Lew Alcindor had scored 37 points and grabbed 20 rebounds. He had done just what everyone had expected: he had led his team to three consecutive NCAA titles. Now it was off to

wards were outstanding, 6ft 7in junior Curtis Rowe and 6ft 9in soph Sidney Wicks. John Vallely was the shooting guard, and a good one, while Henry Bibby was a speedy point guard who could also score.

It was a solid Bruin team, unselfish and balanced, and they must have surprised more than a few people when they checked in with a 24-2 regular-season record. That was good enough to have them rated number two in the country behind Dan Issel and Kentucky. But could they win a fourth straight NCAA title? Their coach, at least, seemed to think they had a chance.

"This team gave me as much satisfaction as any team I coached," Wooden explained. "We had a lot of close games, but they would always find a way to pull them out."

Kentucky, however, wouldn't be the only team challenging for the NCAA title. Notre Dame had a solid club which featured All American Austin Carr. St. Bonaventure, with Lanier, was a threat, and Jacksonville, the surprise team, with 7ft 2in Artis Gilmore, was also considered a title contender: the Dolphins were averaging more than 100 points a game. It looked to be an interesting field, but a crowded one. And that meant good teams would have to knock other good teams off.

For example, in the regional final, Jacksonville upset Kentucky, 106-100, to earn a spot in the Final Four. The Dolphins would be opposed by St. Bonaventure, and everyone was anticipating a Lanier-Gilmore Confrontation. Only it wouldn't happen, because Lanier injured a knee in the East final against Villanova and needed surgery.

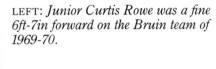

LEFT: *Junior Curtis Rowe was a fine 6ft-7in forward on the Bruin team of 1969-70.*

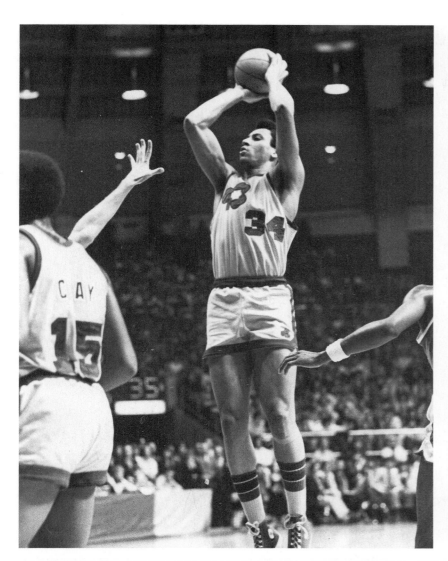

133

OPPOSITE: *At 6ft-11in, Bill Walton was a center who could do it all. He was an especially strong rebounder and one of the best passing centers. His pro career was slowed by injury, but he was good enough to lead the Portland Trailblazers to an NBA crown.*

ABOVE: *UCLA's Larry Hollyfield leans on the 1973 NCAA title trophy. It was the Bruins' seventh straight.*

RIGHT: *North Carolina State and superstar David Thompson would challenge Walton and the Bruins for basketball supremacy in 1973-74.*

game winning streak that would have the basketball world wondering if they would ever lose.

Like most good things, the era of the Walton Gang started slowly in 1971-72. But before long the wins were coming easier, and when the season ended the team was ranked number one and had taken 26 straight games. Not only were the Bruins winning, they were winning by an average margin of 30 points a game. Needless to say, they were overwhelming favorites to make it six straight titles.

Sometimes it seemed that the Walton Gang didn't even break a sweat. That's how easily they won. They reached the NCAA finals against surprising Florida State, took a comfortable 50-39 halftime lead, then coasted to an 81-76 victory, with Walton scoring 24 points and grabbing 20 rebounds. It *was* title number six.

The next year it was more of the same. When the ballclub defeated Loyola of Chicago on January 25, 1973, they had taken their 60th straight victory, tying the record set by Bill Russell's San Francisco team nearly 20 years earlier. And with hardly a pause they set a new mark two nights later by beating Notre Dame. Now the record belonged to the Bruins.

When they reached the NCAA tournament of 1973 the Bruins had the record up to 71 games. They then began their hunt for seven straight titles by beating Arizona State 98-81. In the next round San Francisco tried the old slowdown tactic. It didn't work: the Bruins won

ABOVE LEFT: *At 7ft-4in, N.C. State center Tom Burleson was a big man in the middle. Though not as talented as an Alcindor or a Walton, he still gave Coach Norm Sloan's club the big man all great teams need.*

LEFT: *Burleson and Walton battle underneath as the two clubs meet early in the 1973-74 season. The Bruins won that one 84-66 and would run their winning streak to 88 games before losing to Notre Dame. Then N.C. State would get revenge in the tournament.*

54-39. And guess what? The Bruins were in the Final Four once again.

It wasn't that the competition was bad. In the semifinals that year the Bruins had to play a strong Indiana team, coached by the dynamic Bobby Knight. But they won 70-59, to move into the Finals. There, the Bruins would be meeting Memphis State, a solid team with an outstanding 6ft 9in forward in Larry Kenon and a high-scoring guard in Larry Finch. But on this night, Bill Walton would put on one of the great performances in NCAA history.

The big redhead began going to the basket early, and he just couldn't miss. When it ended Walton had hit on 21 of 22 field goals attempts, for a total of 44 points. And needless to say, the Bruins won yet another championship, 87-66, with Walton taking the MVP prize for the second straight year and keeping the winning streak going at 75 straight.

But there was an unfinished story in 1973. Though ranked number one, the Bruins were not the only unbeaten team that year. The North Carolina State Wolfpack under the leadership of Norm Sloan hadn't lost a single game but couldn't go to the NCAA tournament because of recruiting violations. To many, the team would have been a worthy challenger to UCLA.

The Wolfpack had its own All American superstar in 6ft 4in David Thompson, a ballplayer of unusual qualities. Thompson often seemed to leap to the sky, then hang in the air making all kind of moves before he came down. He was joined by a 7ft 4in center named Tom Burleson. Burleson was nowhere near the complete player Bill Walton was, but he knew how to use his size and always played very hard. The team's third star was 5ft 7in Monte Towe, a speedy guard who set things up for Thompson and Burleson.

In 1973-74 the Wolfpack and Bruins could possibly meet twice. They had a regular-season confrontation already on the schedule, and if both made it to the NCAA tourney they could well meet again, perhaps even in the final round. In addition, the Bruins still had their win streak intact, and with Walton now a senior, it was difficult to envision anyone else winning the national title. If they did that, the Bruins and Coach Wooden would have eight straight.

The Bruins were still a formidable crew. Forward Larry Farmer had graduated, but junior Dave Meyers was ready to step in and take his place. Keith Wilkes was back at the other forward and had become an All America player in his own right. Greg Lee and Tommy Curtis manned the backcourt. When the Walton Gang easily topped Arkansas in the opener 101-79 it looked as if they were off to the races again.

But they had a scare in the next one. Hosting powerful Maryland at the Pauley Pavilion, the Bruins led most of the way, the margin being 65-57 with just a few minutes left. But suddenly the Terrapins came alive and closed the gap to 65-64. Then they got a ball back in the final seconds with a chance to win it. Only a saving block of a John Lucas shot by Dave Meyers enabled the Bruins to win. But it showed other teams that UCLA could be taken.

Two games later came the fateful first meeting with North Carolina State. The game was held on a neutral court in St. Louis, and in the early going the Bruins held the lead. But then Walton got in some foul trouble and had to sit, giving the Wolfpack a chance to get back in it. In the second half the game was tied at 54, but with Walton back the Bruins made a run and wound up winning big, 84-66. So they had beaten back their biggest challenge yet and now looked well on the way to an eighth title.

The victories continued. After 13 victories in 1973-74, the winning streak was at an incredible 88 games, and there was talk of 100 straight victories. But then the Bruin juggernaut traveled to South Bend, Indiana, to do battle with another Digger Phelps' Notre Dame team. The Irish had ended one UCLA winning streak some years earlier and always seemed to play the Bruins tough. But the game seemed to be following the usual pattern, UCLA getting the lead and keeping a comfortable distance between themselves and the Irish. With just three minutes left in the game, the Bruin lead was 70-59. And that's when it happened.

UCLA suddenly went cold – ice cold – while at the same time the Irish began to come on. The Irish scored, then scored again. Walton and company couldn't seem to buy a basket and began making mistakes. It was an incredible turnaround, as Notre Dame reeled off 12 straight points to win the game 71-70 and at the same time end the longest winning streak in the history of the college game.

Some figured the loss would take the pressure off the Bruins and, without having to worry about the streak each night, they would rebound stronger than ever. But it didn't work that way. Four games later they found themselves losing to Oregon State 61-57. Then, in their next game, they were uncerimoniously beaten by a rather average Oregon team 56-51. After that they would rally to win the remainder of their games in time for the NCAA tourney. But now there was a considerable question about their ability to defend their title.

It took them three overtimes to beat Dayton 111-100 in the very first

RIGHT: *"Digger" Phelps' Notre Dame team always gave the Bruins trouble. They ended the longest winning streak in college basketball history in the 1973-4 season by scoring the final 12 points of the game and beating UCLA 71-70.*

137

LEFT: *North Carolina State finally defeated the Bruins in double overtime, 80-77, in the NCAA semifinals. Here, David Thompson wins a battle for the ball with UCLA's Dave Meyers.*

OPPOSITE: *Marques Johnson (54) was still another in the long line of UCLA all-Americans.*

OPPOSITE FAR RIGHT: *Richard Washington (31) helped lead the Bruins to their 10th NCAA title in 1976, a surprise 92-85 victory over Kentucky.*

ABOVE: *Bill Walton is all smiles after receiving the 1973 Sullivan Award as the nation's top amateur athlete. The big redhead had already been named college basketball player of the year for two straight seasons.*

game, and they looked even less like an all-consuming powerhouse. But they won the West Region and headed for the Final Four once again. In the semifinals it would again be North Carolina State. The Wolfpack had come back from their early-season defeat by the Bruins and had wound up the number one-ranked team in the country. Combine that with UCLA's track record in the playoffs, and the game was rated a tossup.

It ended up a classic. Only seven players from each team saw action, as both coaches elected to go with their best. The halftime score was 35-35, with no hint as to which team was going to take charge down the stretch. One thing was certain. Both superstars – Walton and Thompson – were playing brilliant clutch basketball. The fans couldn't have asked for anything more. Towards the end both teams were going to their big men, and they kept producing. When the buzzer sounded the game was still tied, now at 65.

The first OT period resulted in just a single basket for each team, as the defenses wouldn't give an inch. Then, in the second extra session, the Bruins got hot. They shot out to a seven-point lead, the kind of margin the Walton Gang didn't usually lose. But the Wolfpack wouldn't quit. Now it was their turn, and they began to close the gap. Amazingly, they caught and passed the Bruins, and when the buzzer sounded this time, North Carolina State had an 80-77 victory. There would be no eighth straight NCAA for John Wooden's team in 1974.

Bill Walton had scored 29 points and grabbed 18 rebounds against N.C. State, while David Thompson had 28 points and 10 caroms. Years later, when Bill Walton would look back at that season, he still thought his ballclub should have won it.

"We played poorly the last two months of that season," Walton said, in retrospect. "After the win streak we lost four games we should have won. In fact, we should have won 105 in a row. N.C. State had great talent and a gamebreaker in David Thompson, but we had a seven point lead in overtime and made turnovers. We were not as good a team in a slowdown game. Their four-corners slowdown really took us out of it, and I missed a lot of shots around the basket down the stretch."

N.C. State went on to become the new national champion with a

76-64 victory over Marquette in the final, as Thompson led a balanced attack with 21 points. UCLA came back to win the consolation game over Kansas 78-61, but Thompson was named the MVP for the tournament.

For Bill Walton, Keith Wilkes, Greg Lee and the other UCLA seniors it was not a great way to end a career. But the team had been a great one, running up the longest winning streak in college basketball history and winning two NCAA titles. Walton himself proved something of an enigma to those who followed his career. On the court he was close to the perfect player, but off the court he became heavily involved in pressing social issues of the day and was opinionated and outspoken. This made him a subject of considerable controversy and doubtless had the effect of lowering his overall popularity. But as the leader of the Walton Gang he was as good as they come.

Of course, some people had been waiting to see the Bruins fall apart for some time now, and it wasn't thought that Wooden could put together another team to challenge for the top spot in 1974-75. After all, the only returning starter was forward Dave Meyers. There just seemed to be too many holes to fill. But the veteran coach went to work, teaming young Marques Johnson up front with Meyers, installing 6ft 9in Richard Washington in the middle and making Andre McCarter and Peter Trgovich his starting guards. The ballclub managed to win its first 12 games, surprising a lot of people, but in the second half of the season the team faltered a bit, losing on several occasions. So when the NCAA tournament began the Bruins were by no means the overwhelming favorites. In fact, Bobby Knight's Indiana team was the early favorite, the Hoosiers winning their first 28 games. But then star forward Scott May broke his arm, and the loss broke the rhythm of the team. The result was that, contrary to expectations, the Hoosiers never made it to the Final Four.

Once the tournament began UCLA started moving through the West Regionals. Would Wooden's unknown team be a real threat? The question was answered when the Bruins defeated a good Arizona team 89-75, to win the region and once again enter the Final Four. Also surviving the expanded 32-team field were Kentucky, Louisville and

139

ABOVE: *Denny Crum was a John Wooden assistant at UCLA before taking over at Louisville and leading the Cardinals to a couple of NCAA crowns of their own.*

RIGHT: *Richard Washington helped the Bruins beat Denny Crum and Louisville 75-74 in the 1975 NCAA semifinals.*

Syracuse. The Wildcats, now coached by Joe B. Hall, topped the Orangemen in one semifinal, and then the Bruins took to the court against Louisville, coached by longtime Wooden assistant, Denny Crum.

It was a great game, the lead changing hands on numerous occasions, as old master Wooden matched strategies with one of his former allies. With just 48 seconds remaining the Cardinals had a four-point lead and looked ready to defeat the Bruins in their own backyard, since the finals were being held in San Diego. But then perhaps the ghosts of Bruins past intervened, for UCLA got several offensive rebounds before Washington was fouled and hit a pair from the line. Seconds later Marques Johnson stole the ball and went in to score the tying hoop, and the game went into overtime.

Again the two teams battled neck and neck, neither able to put the other away. Then, with just seconds left and Louisville up by a point, Johnson flicked a pass to Washington on the baseline, and the big guy hit a jumper. The Bruins had won, 75-74, and would now meet Kentucky for the championship.

It seemed almost inconceivable that this Bruin team could go all the way. Certainly the Wildcats wouldn't be easy. Coach Hall had an All American in 6ft 5in Kevin Grevey and a pair of 6ft 10in freshmen, Rick Robey and Mike Phillips. Forward Jack "Goose" Givens was also a solid player who could be an explosive scorer.

Once again the game was a close one. Kentucky hung tough until, with less than seven minutes left, there was a big play. The Bruins were up by one, 76-75, when Dave Meyers was called for a charge and, when he protested, a technical. The usually placid Wooden

rushed onto the court and had to be restrained by his aides. Seeing the show of emotion from their coach seemed to light a fire under the Bruins. Kentucky missed the foul shots, and when the Bruins got the ball back they also got the momentum, rushing toward a 92-85 victory behind 28 points from Washington and 24 from Meyers. They had done it again!

It was the tenth national title in 12 years for John Wooden and his Bruins, a mark that will probably never be matched. And after his most surprising and perhaps satisfying win of all, Wooden announced to the basketball world that he was retiring. After all, there were no more worlds to conquer.

For more than a decade the UCLA dynasty had dominated college basketball as no team had before or since. They had done it with a pair of great centers, Lew Alcindor and Bill Walton, but they had also done it without them. John Wooden always said that winning breeds winning, and winning brings more good ballplayers into a program. He certainly proved it at UCLA, making the Final Four his own personal stage. In retirement he remained a respected elder statesman of the game. But he would always be remembered above all as the man who had put together the greatest college basketball dynasty in history. John Wooden, the Wizard of Westwood.

TOP LEFT: *Jack "Goose" Givens was only a freshman when Kentucky lost to UCLA in the 1975 final. Three years later the left forward scored 41 points as the Wildcats won the title with a 94-88 victory over Duke.*

LEFT: *Big Rick Robey was a mainstay of Joe B. Hall's 1978 Kentucky title team.*

ABOVE: *John Wooden and his Bruins celebrate after winning the 1975 championship.*

The Ladies Enter

Women's basketball has by now become a major college sport. Girls today are recruited into basketball programs at the major colleges as intensely as the boys, and the caliber of the women's game has been rising steadily over the past decade and a half. But while women have been playing the court game almost since its invention in 1891, they had always played a different version, with different rules, until standardization took place in 1970.

In basketball's earliest days the women's game was played with nine on a side, with each player confined to a specific area of the court, and the ball had to be passed from area to area before a shot could be taken. Before long the game changed to six players on a side, but it was going in another direction from the men's game. In the six-player version three guards stayed at one end of the court for defense, while the other three players, the forwards, were at the other end to take shots. It was really half-court basketball.

The early women's game also had a rule against dribbling. It was eventually modified to allow a player to bounce the ball once before a pass or shot, but even in the 1950s women were only allowed to bounce the ball twice. And in the 1960s, when the men's game was entering the modern era of greatness, women were only allowed three bounces. It's no wonder the sport had gone nowhere.

Basketball for women actually advanced more in some other countries of the world, where the ladies began playing the men's rules a lot sooner. In 1970 the United States finally dropped from six women on a side to five, but that still didn't make basketball a major college sport for the ladies. That happened only in the mid-1970s, when a new rule was passed that mandated a certain amount of money for women's athletic programs at all colleges and universities receiving federal funds.

What that really meant was that women's teams would now have uniforms, full-time coaches, major schedules and athletic scholarships. Then the game opened up, and after a few pioneer women's players showed what they could do, given the opportunity, girls across the country began to look at the court game in a new way. Soon they began playing, just as the boys did, in summer leagues, pickup games with backyard hoops and in their schools.

To some, the real coming of age for women's basketball occurred in February 1975, when some 12,000 fans paid to see the first women's game ever played at Madison Square Garden. National champion Immaculata College of Pennsylvania played Queens College that night, and the entire evening was introduced by the playing of the song, "I Am Woman." Perhaps someone should have added, "And I can hit a jumpshot, too."

Women may not be as big as their male counterparts, but they have proven very fine basketball players. As in the men's game, the women's game has had its superstars and outstanding players, some who could hit the jumper from anywhere on the court, others who could handle the ball and run the fastbreak. It has become a fast, high scoring game, often played at a breakneck pace.

The NCAA did not start keeping women's records officially until 1982. That's when the first NCAA-sanctioned AIAW national championship tournament began. The AIAW (Association for Intercollegiate Athletics for Women) had in fact begun holding its own title tourney back in 1972, when the women's game really started to take hold and a full decade before the NCAA jumped on the women's bandwagon.

Immaculata won it those first three years. The small women's college in Philadelphia didn't offer any scholarships back then, but it had experienced players from local CYO teams. From 1972 through 1974 Immaculata defeated West Chester State, Queens College and Mississippi College to win its titles. None of those schools would become household names in women's basketball as years passed, but back then they had some of the best teams around.

Immaculata's big advantage was a 5ft 11in center named Theresa Shank, who helped coach Cathy Rush and the Mighty Macs compile a 64-2 record from 1970 to 1974. The team that inherited the championship mantle from Immaculata was Delta State of Mississippi. The Lady Statesmen had a 6ft 3in center in Lucy Harris, who helped her team take the next three AIAW titles through 1977. As in the men's game, the team with the dominant center had an immediate advantage, and Lucy Harris was so good that the New Orleans Jazz made her a pick in the NBA draft.

LEFT: *In the 1980s women's basketball began growing quickly, though women had been playing long before that. The AIAW began holding championship tournaments in 1972, and Immaculata College of Philadelphia won it the first three years, with Coach Cathy Rush at the helm.*

OPPOSITE: *Theresa Shank was an Immaculata star when the rules were standardized and the women began playing a running game similar to the men.*

ABOVE: *Early basketball dress for women.*

RIGHT: *The early women's game: outdoors with no backboard.*

BELOW: *Leila Wirth holds the intramural title trophy at the University of Iowa in 1926.*

ABOVE: *Immaculata's Theresa Shank looks to the hoop during a game in the early 1970s.*

RIGHT: *UCLA's Ann Meyers (left), a basketball all-American.*

BELOW: *Carol Blazejowski of Montclair State was one of the greatest scorers in women's basketball annals. The Blaze scored more than 3000 points and averaged 31.7 a game for four years.*

Scholarships began during this period, and it wasn't long before the big schools were getting into the act. Top players began appearing everywhere. For example, the first woman to receive an athletic scholarship to UCLA was Ann Meyers, the sister of All American Dave Meyers, who had played for several of John Wooden's championship teams. Ann Meyers became a star in her own right, making the All America team four times between 1975 and 1978 and leading the Lady Bruins to the AIAW title in 1978.

The first women's All America team wasn't picked until 1975, and a year later another super player came along and made a major impact on the women's game. Her name was Carol Blazejowski, and she played for Montclair State College in New Jersey. The Blaze was a complete player and one of the most explosive scorers in women's hoop history. She became a three-time All American and was the first to win the Wade Trophy, begun in 1978 and given to the best women's player in the land.

In three years Carol Blazejowski scored 3199 points in just 101 games. That's an average of 31.7 points per contest, still tops for a career women's average, though official NCAA records didn't begin until 1982. While Montclair State never won the AIAW title, the scoring exploits of The Blaze became legendary. In a way, she was the Pete Maravich of women's basketball and showed the kind of offensive game women could play.

Coming in right behind the Blaze was Nancy Lieberman, who quickly became a star at Old Dominion, and Lynette Woodard of Kansas. Both would help the women's game spread throughout the land.

Lieberman had made her mark while still in high school when she became a member of the United States Olympic team. At Old Dominion she ran the offense like any other superstar point guard, man or woman, and led the Norfolk, Virginia, school to the AIAW title in 1979.

145

But more than being a three-time All American and two-time winner of the Wade Trophy, Nancy Lieberman also became a spokesman and pioneer of the women's game.

She would later play a major role in starting a woman's professional basketball league. And though the league eventually folded, Lieberman and others showed that it could work, and it remains a distinct possibility for the future if the women's game continues to grow and spread. In addition to that, Lieberman also had the courage to try out with an NBA team and later played with the touring team that travels with the Harlem Globetrotters. No matter where she is playing, Nancy Lieberman remains a great athlete and ferocious competitor.

Lynette Woodard was simply a great basketball player, a superstar from the day she joined the Kansas team until her final game. She was a four-time All American from 1978-81, and in that time she scored a record 3659 points. In that time she also hit an incredible 52.5 percent of her shots and had a 26.3-point-per-game average.

Other great players who have helped the continued growth of women's basketball include Anne Donovan of Old Dominion, Denise Curry of UCLA, Pam Kelly of Louisiana Tech, Clarissa Davis of Texas, LaTuanya Pollard of Long Beach State, Cheryl Miller of Southern California, Kamie Ethridge of Texas, Shelly Pennefather of Villanova and Sue Wicks of Rutgers.

There are many others, of course, but even this list of outstanding players indicates that they are coming out of schools in all parts of the country. The improved shooting of the women is indicated by game scores that now correspond to men's scores. Thus in 1982 Louisiana Tech won the Division I championship by beating Cheyney 76-62, and in 1986 Texas won in a real shootout over Southern Cal 97-81. Indeed, many of the women's games fall into this range.

In her four years at Southern Cal, Cheryl Miller was in 16 playoff games, scoring 333 points for a 20.8 average. And in a tournament game against Maryland in 1982, Lorri Bauman of Drake had 21 field goals and eight free throws for an incredible 50 points. And there have been a number of 40- and 30-plus point performances. These women

ABOVE LEFT: *College basketball by the 1970s and '80s had become a colorful spectacle. Witness the Louisville cheerleaders and their mascot Cardinal.*

ABOVE RIGHT: *This mascot is a Georgetown Hoya.*

LEFT: *Here, the cheerleaders of two schools join forces.*

OPPOSITE TOP: *Even after 10 NCAA titles, the UCLA Bruins have plenty to cheer about.*

OPPOSITE BOTTOM RIGHT: *Ever a hotbed of basketball, the State of Indiana is proud of its Hoosiers.*

OPPOSITE BOTTOM LEFT: *The Kansas Jayhawks cheerleaders strut their stuff.*

LEFT: *Bobby Knight and his team celebrate Indiana's 86-68 victory over Michigan for the 1976 national championship.*

BELOW LEFT: *In 1977 underdog Marquette defeated North Carolina 67-59, winning the national title and leaving longtime Coach Al McGuire weeping with joy on the bench.*

OPPOSITE: *Jack Givens nails two of his 41 points in the 1978 final that saw Kentucky defeat Duke for the title.*

Because the country was celebrating its Bi-Centennial in 1976, the Final Four was held in the history-rich city of Philadelphia at the modern Spectrum. The first team making it into the finals was speedy Michigan, which defeated the Cinderella Rutgers team 86-70. Then came the big one, Indiana and UCLA. The Hoosiers had beaten the Bruins by 20 points early in the season, but there were still those who thought that UCLA magic would return in the playoffs.

But this time it was Indiana taking control of the game. Knight's club had the balance and the depth, and they weren't about to let the Bruins get into the game. When it ended Indiana had a 65-51 victory and the trip to the finals. For UCLA, well, the Bruins had simply run out of miracles.

The final was anti-climactic. Michigan was no match for its Big Ten rival. The Hoosiers just had too much firepower. They led 35-29 at the half and then really turned it on, winning early, 86-68. May had 26 and Benson 25, with the big center being named the tourney's Most Valuable Player.

It was a significant Final Four in several ways. For one thing, the tourney ended once and for all the UCLA dynasty. The Bruins had given it one more try, but they would now be a team on the downslide for several years. And second, the Indiana victory opened up the NCAA. With UCLA down, every good team in the country knew it had a chance to win the national championship.

The following year it was Marquette that won the tournament, led by guard Butch Lee, upsetting North Carolina 67-59. The Tar Heels had a powerful trio of players in Walter Davis, Mike O'Koren and Phil Ford, yet the underdog Warriors won the game. It was such an emotional night that retiring Marquette coach Al McGuire wept openly on the bench during the final minutes of action when he knew his team would win it. It was a storybook ending to a long and colorful coaching career and the entire country watched it in prime time.

A year later there was a familiar ballclub back on top. The Wildcats of Kentucky became national champs in 1978-79 when they rode home on an unbelievable 41-point performance by forward Jack Givens to take a 94-88 verdict over a very good Duke team led by Gene Banks, Mike Gminski and Jim Spanarkel. The game was something of an upset, and most observers agreed that Kentucky wouldn't have won had not Givens been red hot from start to finish, hitting on 18 of his 27 field goal tries.

During this period there were many other top players entertaining college basketball fans both during the regular season and in the NCAA finals. Some of them were Phil Ford of North Carolina, Otis Birdsong of Houston, David Greenwood of UCLA, Bernard King of Tennessee,

LEFT: *North Carolina's Phil Ford drives to the hoop in a game against archrival North Carolina State. Many intense rivalries arose as the game grew bigger.*

OPPOSITE TOP LEFT: *UCLA's David Greenwood (34) battles Indiana's Kent Benson (54) during the 1976 NCAA semifinals.*

OPPOSITE RIGHT: *Whenever Larry Bird (33) took to the court things happened. The Indiana State forward quickly proved himself one of the best in the country.*

OPPOSITE BOTTOM: *At 6ft-9in, Larry Bird could put the ball on the floor as well as a much smaller guard. Combined with a great outside shot and tenacity under the boards, he was a threat to score from anywhere on the court.*

Mychal Thompson of Minnesota and a blond-haired 6ft 9in forward from unheralded Indiana State University. His name was Larry Bird. While Bird wasn't really well known when the season opened, especially to the casual fan, he was about to burst on the scene as few players before him have.

In fact, before the 1978-79 season ended every basketball fan, no matter how casual, would know the name of Larry Bird. And before the season ended, Bird's name would be linked with another player, a sophomore sensation from Michigan State. The two players' basketball lives would remain intertwined right into the pro ranks. But in 1978-79 they would be the talk of the college basketball world. The other player's name was Earvin Johnson, but everyone called him Magic.

Both players took distinctly different roads to their initial confrontation which, of course, would be at the NCAA championships. Larry Bird was the personification of the smalltown-boy-makes-good story. Born in the little Indiana town of French Lick, Bird had had a difficult childhood. His family was very poor, and one of young Larry's few recreational outlets was basketball. He followed his older brothers onto the courts, but he didn't always have first-class equipment. Sometimes he had to use a rubber ball and a coffee can, but as long as it was basketball it didn't matter.

Because the game was so widespread in Indiana, the youngster learned to play the game correctly, appreciating the team concept and preferring to play with movement and crisp passing, not just hotdog one-on-one. And, fortunately, his coaches right into high school re-

inforced this type of ball.

"The coaches were constantly drilling us on executing the right way," Bird would recall. "It was backdoors, picks and rolls, using the backboard for layups. They kept banging the fundamentals of the game into us. Make a mistake and you did it over. And that was fine with me. I never wanted to leave the court until I got things exactly right. My dream, even then, was to become a pro."

But Bird still had to make a few stops along the way. He was already 6ft 9in when he was graduated high school, and with his great skills he was being recruited by a number of so-called major colleges. Being from Indiana, however, it was no surprise when he opted to play for Bobby Knight. So Bird entered Indiana U in the fall of 1974. But something just didn't feel right for him there, and it wasn't long before he dropped out. He returned home for a brief but unsettled period, then decided to go to Indiana State, which was perhaps a third of the size of Indiana and did not really have a major basketball program. But Larry Bird would change all that – would change it nearly singlehandedly.

For Earvin Johnson home was where the heart was. Born and raised in East Lansing, Michigan, he came from a large family of ten children. He had a close family and hard-working parents, and, like Larry Bird, he followed his older brothers onto the basketball court. He had the disadvantage of always being the youngest kid on the court, so to compensate, he became an outstanding dribbler and ballhandler at an early age.

When he wasn't playing, he was watching, in person or on TV. And when he'd watch the pros in action his father was often right there to point out just how the game should be played.

"My father would point out things like a big guard taking a smaller guard underneath," Magic recalled years later. "Or he would show me how the guys would run a pick and roll. By the time I started playing organized ball, whenever the coach asked if anybody knew how to do a

three-man weave or left-handed layup, I was always the first one up."

So Magic continued to play and improve, and then he started growing. He was no longer the smallest kid on the block, or on the playground, and by the time he was starring at Everett High School, Magic found himself heavily recruited. He ended up following his hometown friend, Jay Vincent, to Michigan State. Since freshman were now allowed to play varsity once again, Magic Johnson became a starter in his first season, 1977-78. At 6ft 8in and still growing, he amazed the basketball world by playing point guard and handling the ball better than most little men. One NBA executive already called him "the most exciting player I've ever seen," adding that "I can't believe that God created a 6ft 8in man who can handle the ball like that."

So the two men continued on their collision course and their date with basketball destiny. Larry Bird was in the process of making Indiana State a court power, and he was made a first team All American following his junior year of 1977-78. Because he had redshirted a year he could have opted for the NBA right then and there. In fact, Red Auerbach of the Boston Celtics drafted him in spite of the fact that Bird said he was planning to return to school. But Auerbach knew he was worth waiting for.

During the 1978-79 season both players were better than ever. Larry Bird averaged 29 points and 15 rebounds, and, with his great passing ability from his forward slot, he also garnered nearly six assists. With Bird leading the way the Sycamores amazed the basketball world by going unbeaten. Although seemingly reluctant to do so, the coaches and writers' polls had little choice but to rank Indiana State as the number one team in the country. Critics kept saying they were a one-man gang and nothing more, so the rest of the club felt they had something to prove as the NCAA championships approached.

For Magic and Michigan State the road was a little more rocky. Center Jay Vincent was injured early on, and the team just couldn't get out of the gate. After 11 games Coach Jud Heathcote's ballclub was a mediocre 6-5 and in the middle of the Big Ten pack. But soon after, Magic and forward Greg Kelser began getting their act together, and the Spartans began winning. In fact, they took 15 of their final 16 games, to finish the season at 21-6. That enabled them to crack the top ten, but they were still a far cry from number one. And with the NCAA tourney again expanding, this time to 40 teams, everyone would have to really hustle to win it.

Indiana State had to win the Missouri Valley tournament to qualify for the NCAAs, but though they won it, Bird broke his thumb in the last game. Thus he was coming into the big one under a handicap, but, being Larry Bird, he simply wrapped the thumb and kept playing.

Indiana State trainer Bob Behnke was one of those who marveled at Bird's determination and tenacity. "Larry is the toughest athlete I've seen in my 16 years in sports," said Behnke. "He could have sat out, but he never gave that a second thought and didn't complain once. And believe me, that thumb hurt."

To be honest about it, the Sycamores *were* close to a one-man team. They had a quality guard in Carl Nicks, but the others were just average ballplayers, and their main job was to try not to make mistakes and to let Bird take care of the tough stuff. In the Midwest Regional semifinal Indiana State beat a good Oklahoma team 93-72, with Bird scoring 29. Like most great ballplayers, his presence seemed to make his teammates raise the level of their game as well.

Now the Sycamores had to face Arkansas and their outstanding All American, Sidney Moncrief. Bird took off like he was shot from a cannon. He scored 25 points in the first 27 minutes, and his club grabbed a big lead. But then the Razorbacks made a defensive change that put the quick 6ft 5in Moncrief on Bird. Moncrief had been told by Coach Eddie Sutton to try to deny Bird the ball. The strategy was sound, and the Razorbacks began cutting the lead. Finally, with less than two minutes remaining, they tied the game at 71-all.

The Razorbacks had a chance to take the lead, but they turned the ball over, giving Indiana State a chance at the last shot. With everyone expecting Bird to get the ball, the Sycamores changed strategy. The pass went to a second-string forward named Bob Heaton, and, incredibly, he canned a shot from the baseline. So Indiana State won the game 73-71, and now they were on their way to the Final Four.

Michigan State, meanwhile, seemed on a roll. They took LSU in the Midwest semis 87-71, with Magic scoring 24 points and adding a dozen assists. Then came a big game with Notre Dame, and sophomore Magic Johnson made it seem as if this would be his final year. "I don't think the team will be back next year," he said. "Kelser is a senior, and me, I don't know what I'm going to do about the pros. So this is it. This is our chance right here."

Against the Fighting Irish the one-two punch of Johnson and Kelser did it again. During one part of the game the 6ft 7in, high-leaping Kelser scored seven straight baskets, and four of them came off nifty passes from Magic. When it ended, Kelser had 34 points, Magic had 13 assists and the Spartans had an 80-68 victory, clearing their way to the Final Four.

At Salt Lake City the draw favored the Spartans. In the semifinals they met a Cinderella Pennsylvania team that really didn't have the guns to compete with them. The Quakers folded their tents early, and the Spartans rolled to a 50-17 halftime lead, before cruising to a 101-67 victory.

Bird and the Sycamores weren't so fortunate. Their semifinal game was against De Paul, the same team that George Mikan had powered so many years before. And the coach was the same. Ray Meyer, who had taught Mikan the game in the 1940s, was now an elder statesman

ABOVE: *Though an all-rounder, Johnson excelled in passing and running the fast break.*

RIGHT: *Arkansas' Sidney Moncrief (32) another ace of the 1970s.*

OPPOSITE: *DePaul's great Mark Aquirre, shown soaring against UCLA, first made his mark as a freshman. He thus helped to keep DePaul in NCAA title contention for four years.*

and the sentimental favorite. He had never won a national championship.

The game was close all the way. And many times during the course of the action it seemed as if it was Larry Bird against the entire De Paul team. Bad thumb and all, the super forward was putting on another incredible show. When De Paul's Gary Garland gave his team a 73-71 lead with five minutes left, De Paul went into a stall. If only they could just keep the ball away from Bird: they still had a 74-73 as time ran down. But once again it was Bob Heaton hitting the key hoop that gave the Sycamores the lead. When De Paul freshman Mark Aguirre missed a shot Indiana got the ball and seconds later the victory. A final free throw made it 76-74, and Larry Bird had wowed everyone again. This time the big guy had had 35 points, making 16 of 19 shots from the floor, and also added a game-high 16 rebounds. There wasn't a soul who doubted his talent now.

So the great meeting was at last set: Indiana State against Michigan State, Larry Bird against Magic Johnson. Coach Heathcote devised a trapping zone defense to contain Bird, and at the same time Johnson and Kelser began making magical music together once more. Indiana State had a chance, because the Spartan defense sent them to the foul line 22 times, but they could convert only ten of them. At the same time, Michigan State got some unexpected late help from guard Terry Donnelly, who hit five long jumpers to stop any late Sycamore run. The final was 75-64, and Michigan State was the national champion.

Magic had finished with 24 points and seven rebounds and won MVP honors. Kelser had 19 and Donnelly 15. For Indiana State, Bird had had a subpar night, with just 19 points. He had hit on only seven of 21 from the floor, thanks to the Spartan defense and perhaps his ever-aching thumb. But it had still been a great season.

With his team reaching the pinnacle, Magic Johnson decided to turn pro the following season, joining the Los Angeles Lakers. Bird justified Red Auerbach's wait and went to the Celtics a year after being drafted. That allowed the two great college rivals resume their confrontations in the pros. But it all started on the hardwood at Salt Lake City in the Final Four.

OPPOSITE: *Guard Carl Nicks of Indiana State was a high-quality player who gave Larry Bird some solid support as the Sycamores made a run at the NCAA title in 1979.*

TOP: *Against Michigan State in the NCAA showdown game, Larry Bird often found himself surrounded by Spartans. Here Jay Vincent (31) and Magic Johnson are on the Bird.*

ABOVE: *When the smoke and fury of 1978-1979 cleared, Coach Jud Heathcote (with ball) and his Michigan State Spartans found that they were the national champions.*

PART V

The Contemporary Game: The Eighties

The Eighties

The 1980's proved to be a great time for college basketball. Outstanding players were in evidence everywhere, and more smaller schools began sending teams to the playoffs. In 1980 Denny Crum and his Louisville Cardinals became national champions. Led by guard Darrell Griffth and forward Rodney McCray, the Cardinals defeated a surprising UCLA team 59-54 in the finals. The Bruins had again peaked in the playoffs after a mediocre regular season, and they had defeated Ray Meyer's number one-ranked De Paul team in the semifinals, again denying the old coach a shot at the title.

In 1981 the number of outstanding players in the college ranks was almost mind-boggling. Indiana had a tremendous guard in Isiah Thomas, while North Carolina had perhaps the best overall front line in college, with Al Wood, James Worthy and Sam Perkins. At the University of Virginia there was a 7ft 4in center named Ralph Sampson who would be the player of the year. De Paul had forwards Mark Aguirre and Terry Cummings, while Brigham Young featured All American guard Danny Ainge. Utah had star forwards Tom Chambers and Danny Vranes, while LSU was led by forward Rudy Macklin. In a year of great forwards, Wichita State had Antoine Carr and Cliff Levingston, Notre Dame had Kelly Tripucka, while centers Steve Johnson of Oregon State and Sam Bowie of Kentucky also attracted notice.

LEFT: *Louisville Cardinal leaper Darrell Griffith.*

ABOVE: *Denny Crum, coach of the Louisville Cardinals.*

OPPOSITE: *Cardinal Freshman Rodney McCray (22) proved he could handle pressure when he helped Louisville win the big one against the Bruins.*

But when the smoke of the playoffs cleared that year a pair of veteran coaches had their teams in the NCAA finals: it was Bobby Knight's Indiana Hoosiers against Dean Smith's North Carolina Tar Heels. Led by 23 points from Isiah Thomas and 11 rebounds from Ray Tolbert, Indiana won it in relatively low-scoring fashion, 63-50. The tournament had a new open format, allowing qualifying small schools to enter, and that sparked interest even more. One other tradition ended when Virginia defeated LSU in the last consolation game played. Perhaps the tourney itself had gotten so big that officials felt a consolation game was anti-climactic.

New players and new contending teams were the order of the day in 1981-82. Georgetown University in Washington, D.C., landed the prize recruit of the year in seven-foot Patrick Ewing. Coach John Thompson had been working to transform the Hoyas into a powerhouse team, and Ewing seemed to be the final piece to the puzzle. He also had an All America-caliber guard in Eric "Sleepy" Floyd and enough intense, talented players to execute his hustling, pressing style of play.

North Carolina was also still a powerhouse and had added a super freshman guard, Michael Jordan, to team featuring big men Worthy and Perkins. In fact, it would be the Tar Heels who would hold down the number-one ranking for most of the season. As long as it had Ralph Sampson, Virginia would be a contender, while a new power was emerging in the Southwest, as the University of Houston had players like Clyde Drexler and Larry Micheaux, as well as a young, seven-foot center from Nigeria named Akeem Olajuwon.

There was a great deal of excitement over the Final Four in 1982, for the games would be played at the huge Superdome in New Orleans. The Superdome, of course, was really a football stadium and had a capacity of more than 60,000. There had only been a few isolated occasions when the game had been played before such big crowds, such as the time UCLA and Alcindor played Houston and Hayes at the Astrodome. But with the championships now being played in such a big arena the tournament seemed to take on even more importance. In fact, some fans point to 1982 as the year the Final Four reached equality with other events such as the World Series and Super Bowl.

The question now was which of the great teams would emerge into the finals. North Carolina was the first. After a couple of close games the Tar Heels topped Villanova to reach the Final Four. Houston was next, beating Boston college. Then Louisville made it, beating little Alabama-Birmingham and giving Denny Crum his second appearance in three years. And the fourth team turned out to be Georgetown. Sent out to the West Regionals, the Hoyas' pressing attack destroyed everyone, including fourth-ranked Oregon State.

With Sam Perkins getting 25 points and ten rebounds, North Carolina whipped Houston 68-63 in one semifinal, while in the other, Georgetown got by Louisville in a bitter battle, 50-46. So it would be a North Carolina-Georgetown final. And, with 61,612 screaming fans at the Superdome, it turned out to be a classic matchup.

The game got off to an unusual and dynamic start. The first four times Carolina came downcourt and shot, freshman Ewing was there to swat the ball away, much to the delight of the huge crowd. But each time he did it the ref ruled goaltending. Ewing was either overexuberant or was that good. But the result was that the Tar Heels had a 8-0 lead without actually making a shot. Once the Hoyas settled down, however, they quickly closed the gap and then took over the lead. The

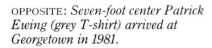

OPPOSITE: *Seven-foot center Patrick Ewing (grey T-shirt) arrived at Georgetown in 1981.*

ABOVE: *Hoya forward Michael Graham (50) listens to Coach John Thompson as Ewing watches.*

RIGHT: *Guard Eric "Sleepy" Floyd is shown here directing the Georgetown attack.*

TOP: *Indiana guard Isiah Thomas (11) would lead the Hoosiers to another national crown in 1981.*

167

LEFT: *At 7ft-4in, Ralph Sampson of Virginia was expected to dominate as Lew Alcindor had done. Though a fine ballplayer, the big guy never saw his Cavaliers win a national championship.*

OPPOSITE LEFT: *North Carolina's Michael Jordan (23) was just a freshman in 1981-82, but he was already a superstar who helped the Tar Heels win it all.*

OPPOSITE RIGHT *Akeem Olajuwon came to Houston via Nigeria. But the seven-footer learned quickly and led the Cougars to the NCAA finals in 1983.*

first half was a battle all the way. Worthy got hot and had 18 points by intermission, but Georgetown still held a 32-31 lead.

In the second half the lead continued to change hands, as neither team could open it up. It became obvious that this one was going to go right down to the wire. With six minutes left, Worthy converted two free throws to put his team on top 57-56. Minutes later the lead was three, but then Ewing hit a short jumper to cut it to one, at 61-60. With less than a minute left Sleepy Floyd hit a jumper to give Georgetown the lead, 62-61. Carolina worked for the final shot, and with just 15 seconds left, freshman Jordan calmly sank a 15-footer from the left baseline. 63-62.

The Hoyas tried to break back quickly. Guard Fred Brown dribbled the ball over the halfcourt line and then thought he saw a teammate alongside him. He quickly passed the ball. But the supposed teammate turned out to be Carolina's James Worthy. That did it: though Worthy would miss a pair of last-second free throws, the Hoyas couldn't score, and the Tar Heels were national champs by a single point.

Amidst all the excitement and celebration by North Carolina, the camera caught a dramatic shot of Coach Thompson hugging the disconsolate Brown, who had made the fatal gaff. It was a dramatic sidelight that added impact to an already amazing game and telecast.

The next year there was an odds-on favorite before the tournament began. It was the Houston Cougars, a team that seemed to be getting

stronger and stronger. With Akeem Alajuwon becoming a major force in the middle, Coach Guy Lewis had a team of dunking demons known as "Phi Slamma Jamma." The team was 27-2 during the regular season and was favored to take the title. But the 1983 tourney would wind up falling to another, a true Cinderella ballclub.

They were the North Carolina State Wolfpack. This was not nearly the same kind of dominant N.C. State team as the Thompson-Burleson-Towe ballclub that had upended UCLA nearly a decade earlier. This was, in fact, just a better than average team that was 20-10 in the regular season. Yet with the charismatic, loquacious Jim Valvano behind the bench, anything could happen. And it started to happen in the Atlantic Coast Conference tournament when the Wolfpack upset both North Carolina and Virginia to win the conference crown and gain a berth in the NCAA playoffs.

Had they not won that conference tourney, there's certainly little chance that the Wolfpack would have received a bid to the NCAAs. Once there, however, the Wolfpack began playing great basketball. Most of their games were close, but they always seemed to find a way to win. First, they reached the Final Four, then tripped up another surprise team, Georgia, winning 67-60. In the other semifinal Houston rode a 21-point, 22-rebound, eight-blocked-shot performance by Akeem Olajuwon to defeat Louisville 94-81. The Cougars were immediate heavy favorites to win the title.

ABOVE: *North Carolina State's Lorenzo Charles jams home an air ball to give Coach Jim Valvano's Wolfpack a last-second 54-52 victory over Houston for the 1983 national title.*

ABOVE RIGHT: *Akeem Olajuwon goes high to block a Louisville shot during 1983 semifinal action.*

RIGHT: *NCAA tournament games had become major media events by the 1980s. Sport, pagentry and endless interviews were all grist for the TV mills.*

OPPOSITE: *Kentucky's Sam Bowie, a talented seven-footer who often made life tough for opponents under the backboards.*

The 1983-84 season was another year of the big man. Ewing was still at Georgetown, and Olajuwon was at Houston. They seemed to be the top two, but Kentucky had its twin towers of 7ft 1in Sam Bowie and 6ft 11in Mel Turpin, and a number of other schools also had big guys dominating the middle.

As the season progressed, it began to look more and more as if it might be Georgetown's year. John Thompson had an intimidating team that didn't give opponents the chance to get into their game. In addition to Ewing the ballclub was filled with top personnel and role players, with everything choreographed by Coach Thompson. Michael Jackson

was a slick point guard who worked extremely well with Ewing. David Wingate was the shooting guard, while Gene Smith was used as a defensive specialist. The starting forwards were often the tough 6ft 9in Michael Graham and 6ft 7in freshman Reggie Williams, who could really put the ball in the hoop. Bill Martin was a solid backup at forward, and Fred Brown, who had thrown the disastrous pass two years earlier, was also back.

Playing in the Big East Conference, which had become extremely tough and competitive, the Hoyas had put together a 29-3 mark during the regular season. Yet come playoff time they were sent to the West

Regional, where they had a close game with SMU before rolling over Nevada Las Vegas and Dayton to earn their ticket to Seattle for the Final Four.

The Hoyas, of course, were led by the intimidating Ewing, and two of the three other final entrants were schools that had big men sitting in the middle. Kentucky, with Bowie and Turpin, had made it by taking Illinois in the regional final. Houston, with Olajuwon, had taken the Midwest with a final victory over Wake Forest. The surprise team was Virginia. The Cavaliers no longer had Ralph Sampson, yet they had defeated several good teams to earn their trip to Seattle.

Knowing they couldn't compete with the size of the other schools, Virginia played a stalling game against Houston. Somehow the Cavaliers managed to tie it in regulation, but Houston came through in the overtime to take the victory. Then came the Kentucky-Georgetown game, a contest still talked about in Wildcat and Hoya basketball circles.

Kentucky came roaring out of the gate and raced to a 27-15 lead after the first 11 minutes. In the process, they had put Ewing on the bench with three fouls and looked to be in almost total control of the game. Coach Thompson knew he had to do something, so he called for his

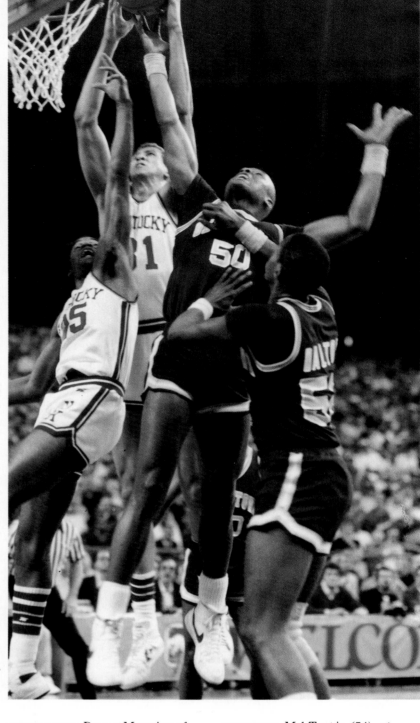

team to press. The strategy worked, and by halftime Georgetown had cut the lead to 29-22.

In the second half, while the Hoyas had come out with fire in their eyes, the Wildcats seemed half asleep. They folded up like a house of cards, failing to score the first 14 times they had the ball during the second half. They went a full ten minutes, the equivalent of a quarter, without getting a hoop. Georgetown moved on top 34-29 before Kentucky scored at all, then ran off 11 more to make it 45-31. Kentucky never did come alive, and the Hoyas coasted in from there, winning by a 53-40 final.

In the second half of the action the Wildcats had hit on just three of 33 field goal tries. Even worse, in the final 20 minutes their five starters missed all 21 shots they tried. It was perhaps the most dramatic mid-game turnaround in NCAA history. Now the Hoyas would have to keep the momentum going against Houston, which had Akeem Olajuwon as its great equalizer.

The game followed the same basic script. Houston jumped in front early, running up a 10-2 lead in the early going. But then Georgetown stormed back. Wingate and Williams were doing most of the scoring, while Ewing and Graham took care of business in the hole. Olajuwon was the one with foul trouble in this one, and, with the big guy on the bench part of the time, Georgetown was able to take a 40-30 halftime lead.

Maybe it was fouls that really won this one. When Olajuwon drew his fourth personal just 23 seconds into the second half, Georgetown was in command. Houston battled back, closing to four, then three at

ABOVE LEFT: *Danny Manning of Kansas deflects a shot by Hoya Charles Smith.*

ABOVE RIGHT: *Hoya Mike Graham (50) and Bowie go for a rebound.*

OPPOSITE: *Mel Turpin (54), at 6ft-11in, joined forces with seven-footer Sam Bowie to give the Kentucky Wildcats a pair of Twin Towers up front.*

57-54, but that was as close as they got. The Hoyas took command underneath again and went on to take their first national championship 84-75. Reggie Williams scored 19 points, and Ewing was the Most Valuable Player. Since attendance in Seattle's Kingdome for the final was 38,471, the game again showed that it could attract big crowds in stadiums that were primarily designed for football.

Even before the smoke from the 1984 final had cleared Georgetown was being touted as the favorite for the following year. After all, Coach Thompson would have Patrick Ewing back one more time, and there seemed to be talent all the way down the bench. In fact, however, the entire Big East was one of the strongest conferences in the country. Besides Georgetown, both Syracuse and St. John's had outstanding teams, and some of the others weren't far behind. But little did anyone know that it would be another Big East team altogether that would emerge as the Cinderella ballclub of the 1985 NCAA tournament.

It proved to be a real Big East convention when the NCAA playoffs moved into the Rupp Arena in Lexington. Georgetown was there, as expected, and was the big favorite to repeat. In the semifinals the Hoyas would be meeting Big East rival St. John's, a team featuring All

Americans Chris Mullin and Walter Berry, and a ballclub that had beaten the Hoyas in the regular season, grabbing the number one ranking for several weeks. The other semifinal would have Memphis State, with big men Keith Lee and William Bedford, going against the Cinderella team. That team was the Villanova Wildcats of Coach Rollie Massimino.

It was the first time ever that one conference had sent three teams to the Final Four, and the third one was certainly a surprise. In the regular season Villanova had just a 19-10 record, usually not good enough for an invitation. But because the Wildcats had competed in the tough Big East they received an at-large bid to the tourney and had made the most of their opportunity, upsetting several teams on their way to the Final Four.

In one semifinal Georgetown avenged its earlier defeat by routing St. John's 77-59, as Reggie Williams scored 20 and Ewing added 16. And by beating the Redmen to make it into the final the Hoyas had looked all but invincible. To many it didn't really matter who won the other semi, though Memphis State, with its two big men, might stand the better chance against John Thompson's team.

But Villanova wasn't about to close up shop without a fight. The Wildcats took it right to Memphis State and came away with yet another surprise win, this one by a 52-45 count. Now they would go up against Big East rival Georgetown for all the marbles. Even the Wildcats' ebullient coach, Rollie Massimino, wondered publically if his team really had a chance to win. "To win it, we've really got to play a perfect game," he said, "and even that might not be enough. We can't let their pressure defense force turnovers, and we'll have to shoot 50 percent or better."

There weren't too many people in the Wildcats' corner when they took the court against the Hoyas. Yet in the early going Georgetown wasn't really making any kind of headway, let alone looking like they were going to blow Villanova off the court. On the contrary, it was the Wildcats who looked calm and confident, hitting shots from all over the court. Whenever Georgetown went into its feared press, point guard Gary McLain seemed able to break it almost effortlessly with his deft dribbling.

TOP LEFT: *Walter Berry (21) of St. John's.*

TOP RIGHT: *Georgetown's forward Reggie Williams (shooting).*

ABOVE: *Another St. John's all-American, Chris Mullin.*

OPPOSITE: *Hoya Patrick Ewing flies through the air.*

RIGHT: *Villanova's John Pinckney (54) was one of the stars of the Wildcats' surprise 1985 run at the NCAA title. In the all-Big East final against Georgetown, Pinckney played against Ewing, and Villanova won it, 66-64.*

OPPOSITE TOP: *Rollie Massimino, Villanova's emotional coach, was sometimes a one-man show on the bench. But he coached, urged, plotted, begged and willed his Wildcats to a national title.*

OPPOSITE BOTTOM: *Tourney MVP Ed Pinckney leads a wild celebration in Philadelphia after Villanova brought home the national championship in one of the great upsets of all time.*

The other Wildcat starters – Harold Pressley, Dwayne McClain, Harold Jensen and Ed Pinckney – were more than holding their own with the mighty Hoyas. The 6ft 9in Pinckney was also playing Ewing to a standoff inside, both in scoring and on the boards. It was a real battle in the opening 20 minutes, and when the buzzer sounded the surprising Wildcats had a one-point lead at 29-28.

As the second half got underway most of the crowd of more than 23,000 fans seemed to be waiting for Georgetown to explode and run the Wildcats off the court. But the waiting continued, for it seemed that every time a Villanova player took a shot it went in. The Wildcats built their lead to 36-30, then, a little while later, they still held the advantage at 53-48. They couldn't shake the Hoyas, but they weren't allowing them to catch up, either.

Then, suddenly, the incessant Georgetown pressure seemed finally to turn the tide. The Wildcats turned the ball over several times, and the Hoyas sprinted into the lead 54-53. With some four minutes left, it looked as if Georgetown had finally made its move.

But Villanova refused to lose. A Georgetown turnover gave the Wildcats the ball, and seconds later they had the lead again. That's the way they played it right down to the buzzer. They hit every important shot and frustrated Georgetown time and again. When the buzzer sounded Villanova still had only that slim lead, 66-64, but now the game was over. They had won it.

The statistics were almost unbelievable. The Wildcats had hit on 78.6 percent of their shots from the field, and in the second half they had connected on an incredible 90 percent. Harold Jensen, for in-

stance, hit on all five of the long jumpers he took in the second half. Pinckney was named the MVP, having scored 16 points and grabbed six rebounds in the final. But the Villanova victory was really a tribute to the total team effort and to a coach who just wouldn't let his guys fold under tremendous pressure. It was also another feather in the cap of the NCAA tournament.

Once again there was a changing of the guard. The Ewing era was over when the big guy from Georgetown went to join the New York Knicks of the NBA. With Akeem Olajuwon having left the previous year, the two dominant big men were gone. So were several other All Americans who had been making headlines for the past several years. But they had all done their job of making the college court game bigger and better than ever, and the NCAA reaped the reward in 1986 by expanding the tournament field to 64 teams. Although some thought the tourney might be getting too big, the majority of fans seemed to enjoy the larger field and the chance to see more teams, and the expansion went well.

Duke, with its slick All America guard, Johnny Dawkins, leading the way, was the number one team for the most of the 1985-86 season. The Blue Devils were 28-2 for the year and were the early favorites to win the big one. Thus no one was particularly surprised when the Blue Devils swept through four straight playoff opponents to make it to the Final Four. In those games Dawkins scored 27, 25, 25 and 28 points. The first two playoff wins for Duke were over Mississippi Valley State and Old Dominion. That, in itself, clearly showed the result of the expanded field. Years earlier small schools such as those could never have hoped to get into the tournament.

Other Final Four teams in 1986 were Louisville, LSU and Kansas. Denny Crum's Cardinals won one semifinal 88-77 over LSU, while Duke stayed true to form in the second, topping Kansas 71-67 behind

179

ABOVE LEFT: *In 1986 freshman center Pervis Ellison led Louisville to another national title, as the Cards topped Duke in the final. Ellison scored 25 and lived up to his nickname, "Never Nervous."*

ABOVE RIGHT: *Guard Milt Wagner was another mainstay for Coach Denny Crum's Cardinals.*

RIGHT: *Senior forward Billy Thompson (55) had 22 points in Louisville's 88-77 semifinal victory over Louisiana State.*

OPPOSITE: *Duke's all-American guard, Johnny Dawkins, sparkled in 1985 and scored 24 points in the final game, but it wasn't enough to bring the Blue Devils a title.*

24 Dawkins points. Coach Mike Krzyzewski's Blue Devils were still installed as favorites to take it all, but Louisville had a fine forward in senior Billy Thompson and a good senior guard in Milt Wagner, and the key to the team was a 6ft 9in freshman center, Pervis Ellison, whose nickname was "Never Nervous."

Having learned his trade at the side of John Wooden, Denny Crum always had his teams ready, and it became apparent soon after the game started that the talented Duke team was not going to win in a walk. Ellison was controlling the game on the inside, and the first half was extremely close: at halftime Duke held only a 37-34 lead.

It stayed equally close during most of the second half. Finally, it was the young Louisville center, living up to his nickname, who made the

difference. Ellison was indeed never nervous. With four minutes left he worked his way inside to score the go-ahead hoop. Louisville now led 63-62 and continued to hold the one-point margin, at 66-65, when there was 2:40 left on the clock. At that point Crum ordered a stall, and his ballclub ran the clock down to 40 seconds. And when the Cardinals' Jeff Hall threw up an airball Ellison was there to grab it and toss it down, giving Louisville a three-point lead at 68-65. The Cards were able to hang on from there, winning 72-69 and giving Coach Crum national title number two. Ellison, with 25 points and 11 rebounds, took the MVP prize. Dawkins finished with 24 and probably would have been the MVP if his team had come out on top.

The big news in 1986-87 was a major rule change. The college game

181

followed the pros by several years in instituting a three-point field goal. Any shot made good from beyond 19 feet, six inches would yield three points instead of two. Officials hoped that the new rule would bring more excitement to the game, allowing a team to gain ground faster and bringing the little men into the game. Now teams would benefit by having guards who could hit consistently from behind that three-point line, and the whole game wouldn't be played inside the paint up front.

There was little doubt that the three-point rule changed strategy and the outcome of some games, and in fact, it would play a prominent role in the NCAA final that year. Yet for much of the season a great deal of news was still being made by a big man. He was 7ft 1in center David Robinson, and he performed on an unlikely stage: he played for the Naval Academy, a school that had never really been known for its basketball program.

Robinson was actually taller than the height limit for naval cadets, but when he entered the Academy as a freshman he hadn't grown to his full height. But as he grew it also quickly became obvious that he was a very great basketball player. Robinson seemed to have all the

qualities that make for a superstar center: he could score, rebound, block shots and run the floor. And while Robinson might have been the only class A player on the Navy team, whenever he was in the lineup the team was dangerous. By virtue of some outstanding performances in his final two years he helped Navy engineer some stunning upsets, and he finished third in the nation in scoring, with a 28.2 average, and fourth in rebounding, with 11.8 a game.

The three-point shot made its presence felt in the NCAA playoffs when two of the Final Four teams were clubs that had thrived on it all year. The first was a surprise entry, Providence College from the Big East. The Friars were a team with neither a truly big man nor anyone who could be called a superstar. But they were a ballclub that could hit the long jumper, and they won that way all season, especially in the playoffs.

Then there were the Runnin' Rebels of Nevada-Las Vegas. Coach Jerry Tarkanian had a guard named Freddie Banks who could fire from deep, but he also had a big man, Armon Gilliam, who played tough underneath. The third team, Bobby Knight's Indiana Hoosiers, also

OPPOSITE: *Navy center David Robinson was the 1987 Player of the Year. The seven-footer's military obligation, however, will delay the start of his pro career.*

LEFT: *In play, Robinson evoked memories of Alcindor, Walton, Ewing and Olajuwon.*

ABOVE: *The fiery Rick Patino led the Providence Friars to a surprise Final Four appearance in 1987. There, the Cinderella team bowed to Big East rival Syracuse.*

183

LEFT: *Syracuse center Rony Seikaly's (4) tough play underneath led the Orangemen to a 67-53 victory over Boston College in the Big East tournament's quarter final round.*

BELOW: *Danny Manning of Kansas became college basketball's best player in 1988. At 6ft-11in, Manning was already being called a taller Magic Johnson, and he didn't disappoint, leading the Jayhawks to an NCAA title.*

OPPOSITE: *Indiana's Keith Smart (23) came on to score 23 points in the Hoosiers 74-73 victory over Syracuse for the 1987 NCAA title. Four players did all the scoring for Indiana, but three of them had 20 or more points.*

had a three-point threat in All American Steve Alford, though no one could ever be sure of Knight's game plan. Only the fourth finalist, Syracuse, really wasn't a threat to hit from way out, and that deficiency had hurt them on and off during the regular season.

With the finals once again being played indoors, this time in the New Orleans Superdome, there would be perhaps 65,000 fans checking out the new three-point rule. In the first semifinal the two Big East teams – Providence and Syracuse – got set to do battle. Jim Boeheim's Syracuse Orangemen were a solid team from point guard Sherman Douglas to center Rony Seikaly. Throughout the game they kept a pretty good lid on Rick Patino's sharpshooters and managed to keep the three-point shot from being much of a factor. The result was a 77-63 victory, ending the Friars' Cinderella run and putting the Orangemen in the final.

In the second game the fans saw a real shootout. Nevada-Las Vegas always seemed to have a team that could score, and this one was no exception. Banks scored 38 points, including a brace of three-pointers, while Gilliam popped for 32 inside. But the Runnin' Rebels still lost to Indiana 97-93, as Alford scored 33 and had plenty of help from his Hoosier teammates. So that set up the final between Indiana and Syracuse.

Once again the final was a close, exciting game, not decided until the final seconds. The Orangemen took the lead early behind the fine play of center Seikaly, but Indiana soon stormed back. Alford seemed intent on taking three-point shots, and he was making them, yet it was a one-point game at the half, Indiana up, 34-33.

It stayed close during the second half. Then, in the final seconds, Syracuse went ahead by one, 74-73. But Indiana had the last shot. The ball went to Keith Smart on the baseline, and he hit it, giving the Hoosiers a 74-73 victory and Bobby Knight his third national championship.

In many ways it was a strange game. Douglas had 20 and Seikaly 18 for the Orangemen. Indiana, with nine men seeing action, had only four scorers, but three of them had 20 points or more. Steve Alford led the way with 23, and in doing so, he showed the basketball world just what the three-point shot could do. Alford was eight for 15 from the floor, but he was seven of ten from beyond three-point range. Had those seven hoops counted only two points, Syracuse would have won the title.

There was more drama in 1988, but this time the plot was a bit different. It involved one super player carrying an entire team to the national championship. Again it was the story of an underdog rising to the occasion in what has become the biggest basketball event in the world.

The player was Danny Manning, and the school was the University of Kansas, the same Jayhawks who were once coached by James Naismith and then Phog Allen. Now the coach was Larry Brown, a former North Carolina player, professional star and itinerant coach. Brown's coaching career seemed to see-saw from the college to pro ranks, from such diverse programs as the New Jersey Nets and UCLA. But in 1988 he was at Kansas, and in Manning many felt he had the best player in the country.

185

Manning was a 6ft 11in forward whom many called a taller Magic Johnson. By that they meant that he could handle the ball as well as smaller men, yet go inside and work the boards, and that he could score from anywhere. The son of former pro player Ed Manning, who was one of Brown's assistants, Danny Manning had such rave advance notices that some felt he could never live up to them.

Yet Manning was a second-team All American as a sophomore in 1986, then a first-team selection the following year, averaging 23.9 points a game. In 1987 the Jayhawks finished at 25-11 and were not a top ten team, though they won several NCAA games before being eliminated by Georgetown in the regional semifinal. There was even some speculation that Manning might turn professional following his junior year, but he decided to finish his career at Kansas.

Unfortunately, the Jayhawks were not really a powerhouse team in 1988, and Manning again had much of the responsibility of carrying the ballclub on his shoulders. During the regular season the team lost 11 times and weren't sure of an NCAA bid. But they got it, and once the team began playing its tournament games the real Danny Manning stood up. Did he ever!

He started taking charge in the preliminary games when the Jayhawks topped Xavier of Ohio 85-72 Murray State in a tight one, 61-58, and then Vanderbilt, 70-64. The Jayhawks still didn't look overpowering at this point, but they were winning, and Manning was throwing in about 27 points a game. Then came the Midwest regional final, with a lot of pride at stake as the Jayhawks went up against cross-state rival Kansas State. The winner would not only earn bragging rights in the

BELOW: *The much-traveled Larry Brown coached Kansas to the 1988 national championship. Coaching in both the pro and college ranks, Brown has always been a winner, though a winner who seems to enjoy moving around. The year after winning the NCAA title, he moved back to coaching in the NBA.*

RIGHT: *Danny Manning proved a clutch performer for Kansas down the stretch. It was a perfect example of a great player raising his game to an even higher level when the NCAA title was on the line.*

OPPOSITE: *Steve Alford (12) of Indiana showed the value of the new three-point shot rule in the 1987 title game when he canned seven three-point baskets and finished with 23 points.*

state, but would also be headed for the Final Four, and the site for the tournament was nearby Kansas City.

This was the game in which Manning and his Jayhawk teammates really began asserting themselves, winning it 71-58, in what was considered a mild upset. Now they were in the Final Four and would be meeting a very tough Duke team in the semifinal. The Jayhawks were still very much the underdogs, but Coach Brown's game plans were good ones, and whenever the team got into trouble it could usually rely on Manning to save the day. That's what happened against Duke. Manning scored 25 points, including a number of the clutch variety, and the Jayhawks won 66-59, earning their way into the final.

Waiting for them were the Sooners of Oklahoma, perhaps the most explosive team in the country. Coach Billy Tubbs' team seemed to make a habit of cracking the 100-point mark, and they were a team that put tremendous pressure on their opponents at both ends of the court.

In Harvey Grant and Stacy King, the Sooners had a pair of All American-caliber players. But the Jayhawks had Danny Manning.

Whenever the Sooners looked as if they were making a run Manning would get a key hoop, or a big rebound, or block a shot or make a steal. He was doing it all, *à la* Magic Johnson, and he was doing it on the biggest college stage of all. It was really a case of a great player reaching his full potential at just the right time.

Kansas took the lead for good in the second half, and the Sooner offense seemed to sputter. Oklahoma stopped getting the ball to Grant, and at the other end they couldn't stop Manning. Though exhausted in the final minutes, Manning still got the key baskets that gave Kansas another national championship, 83-79. The Jayhawks' victory continued the trend of big NCAA upsets during the 1980s: the tournament had really become a wide-open, up-for-grabs affair.

As for Danny Manning, he had scored 31 points in the final game,

leaving his average at 27.2 for the six NCAA tournament contests. He would be college basketball's Player of the Year and subsequently the number one choice in the National Basketball Association draft.

Milt Newton was the next Jayhawk scorer, with 15, while Dave Siegar had 22, King 17 and Grant 14 for the Sooners. But Manning was the big story and perhaps even provided a glimpse of the future, as had Magic Johnson before him. At 6ft 11in, Manning could do many of the things formerly reserved for smaller men. He was a far cry from the 6ft 10in George Mikan who, half a century earlier, had had to work so hard once he reached college to just learn some of the fundamentals of the game. To the great players of today, such things are second nature.

With so many great players continuing to come into the college ranks there is no reason to think that college basketball won't continue to grow, both in quality and quantity. With its big 64-team tournament the NCAA now offers almost every school with a good team a chance to go for the glory. One of these years perhaps one of the small schools will write the ultimate Cinderella story.

Until then, the fans will continue to flock to the gyms, field houses, and arenas all around the country to watch their favorite teams perform. Cable television has enabled more games than ever to be beamed into homes in every corner of the land. There is no reason, then, to think that the 1990s won't be greater than ever.

Of course, the game still isn't perfect. The competition for top players and high rankings will always make it necessary for the NCAA to watch recruiting practices – and even the games themselves, for there is still that point spread to tempt the wrong kind of people.

But at least no one can now doubt that the sport is definitely major league. It has its history and traditions, and names like Mikan, Kurland, Gola, Russell, Chamberlain, Robertson, West, Alcindor, Walton, Bird, Johnson and Manning all mean something to the knowledgable fan. For a sport that was begun for casual recreation, basketball has come a long way. And it is still the perfect winter game to elicit pride and create excitement among men and women in colleges and universities everywhere across the land.

189

INDEX

Numbers in *italics* indicate illustrations

Abernathy, Tom 148
Aguirre, Mark *159*, 161, 164
Ainge, Danny 164
Akron College 81
Alabama, University of 148
Alabama-Birmingham 167
Alcindor, Lew 116, 120, *120*, 121, 124, 125, *125*, 126, *127*, 129, 131, 132, 141, 148, 167, 189
Alford, Steve 184, 185, *187*
Allen, Forrest 'Phog' *15*, *56*, 56, 81, 88, 98, 185
Allen, Lucius 124, 125, 126, *126*
Amateur Athletic Union 20, 28, 40, 61
Amherst College 18
Anet, Bobby 45
Arizin, Paul 80
Arizona State 136, 139
Arkansas State Teachers College *19*
Arkansas, University of 60, 70, 137, 158
Armory Hill YMCA *11*
Armory, Patterson, N.J. *24*
Army. *See* United States Military Academy at West Point
Associated Press 73, 74, 75
Association for Intercollegiate Athletics for Women (AIAW) 142, 146
Astrodome 167
Auerbach, Red 156, 161

'Badgers'. *See* Wisconsin, University of
Banks, Freddie 183, 184
Banks, Gene 152
Barker, Cliff 70
Barnstable, Dale *84*, 85
Barry, Rick 120
Bartow, Gene 148
Basketball Hall of Fame 86
Bauman, Lorri 146
Baylor, Elgin 86, *101*, 101, 102
Baylor University 61, 70, 78
'Bearcats'. *See* Cincinnati, University of
Beard, Ralph 64, 66, *74*, *69*, 70, 74, 75, *84*, 85
'Beavers'. *See* City College of New York (CCNY)
Bedford, William 176
Bee, Clair *37*, 37, *42*, 42, *43*, 43, 47, *83*, 84
Begovich, Matty 30, *30*
Behnke, Bob 158
Bellamy, Walt 108, *112*, 112
Bemies, Charles O. 17
Bender, Julie *37*, 37
Bennett, Wes 34, 35
Benson, Ken 148, *148*, 152, *155*
Berenson, Sandra *14*
Berry, Walter 176, *176*
Bibby, Henry 130, *131*
'Big E'. *See* Hayes Elvin
Big East Conference 172
Big Ten 18, 47, 57, 156
Bigos, Adolph *83*
'Billikins'. *See* St. Louis University
Bird, Larry *7*, 7, 19, *113*, 154, *155*, 155, *156*, 156, 158, 161, 189
Birdsong, Otis 152
'Blackbirds'. *See* Long Island, University of
'Black Sox' scandal 80, 85
Blazejowski, Carol 145, *145*
'Blue Demons'. *See* DePaul University
'Blue Devils'. *See* Duke University
'Bobcats'. *See* Montana State
Bobham, Ron 108
Boeheim, Jim 184
Boryla, Vince 75
Boston Celtics 98, 156, 161
Boston College 167, *167*, *184*
Bowie, Sam 164, 172, 173, *173*, 174, 175
Bowling Green University *57*, 57, 112, *113*
Boykoff, Harry 51, *52*, 52
Bradley 41, *76*, 76, *78*, 78, 83, 85, 94, *112*, 112
Bradley, Bill *116*, 116, 120
Bradds, Gary *123*
'Braves'. *See* Bradley
Brennan, Pete 100
Brigham Young University 86, 119, 164
Broberg, Gus 47
Bromberg, Johnny *37*, 42, 43
Brookfield, Price 48
Brooklyn, E.District 'Y' 14
Brooklyn Central 14
Brooklyn College 81
Brooklyn College of Pharmacy 37
Brooklyn Jewels 33
Brown, Fred 169, 172
Brown, Larry 185, 186, *186*, 188
'Bruins'. *See* California, University at Los Angeles, (UCLA)
'Buckeyes'. *See* Ohio State
Bucknell University 19
Buckner, Quinn 148, *149*
'Buffalos'. *See* Colorado, University of
Bunn, John 38
Burleson, Tom *136*, 137
Burrows, Pembroke 131

'Cadets'. *See* United States Military Academy at West Point
Cager, Willie 122
Caldewood, Jack *38*
California Aggies *112*
California, University at Los Angeles, (UCLA) 78, 94, 110, 116, *119*, 120, 121, 124, 125, 126, *126*, 129, 130, 131, 132, *133*, 136, 137, 138, 139, 140, *141*, 141, 145, 146, 148, *151*, 152, *155*, *159*, 164, 167, 169, 185
California, University of Southern (USC) 61, 80, 94, 103, 107, 108, 119, 124, 125, 126, 146
Calverly, Ernie *64*, 64
Canisius 53
Cann, Howard 28, *30*
'Cardinals'. *See* Louisville, University of
Carr, Antoine 164
Carr, Austin 130, 132, *133*
'Cavaliers'. *See* Virginia, University of
Chamberlain, Wilt *63*, 86, *98*, 98, *99*, 99, *100*, 100, 101, 102, 105, 189
Chambers, Jerry 124
Chambers, Tom 164
Chappell, Len 112
Charles, Lorenzo 170, *172*
Cheyney 146
Chicago, University of 16, 17, 18, 19, *25*
Chicago White Sox 80
Cincinnati, University of 102, 103, 107, *108*, 108, *109*, 110, 112, 116, 122
Cincinnati Reds 80
City College of New York (CCNY) 28, 30, 32, 34, 35, *36*, 37, 64, *74*, 75, *75*, *76*, 76, *78*, 78, *79*, 80, 83, 84, 85
Clark, John Kirkland 18
Coffey, John F. *69*
Cohen, Herb *74*, 85
Colgate University 64
Colorado, University of *41*, 41, 47, *96*, 96
Columbia University 18, 19, 20, 27, 32, 70
Cornell University 18
Costello, Larry 94
'Cougars'. *See* Houston, University of
Cousy, Bob 64, *66*, 70, 80, *91*
Crnokrak, John *84*
Crum, Denny *140*, 140, 164, *164*, 167, 179, 181
'Crusaders'. *See* Holy Cross College
Cummings, Terry 164
Curry, Denise 146
Curtis, Tommy 137

Dallmar, Howard 48
Dambrot, Irwin *74*, 75, 76, *77*, 78, 85
Dampier, Louie *121*, 122
Daniel, Dan 33
Daniels, Mel 129
Dartmouth College 18, 47, 48, *54*, *55*, 55
Davidson 120
Davies, Bob *44*, 47
Davis, Clarissa 146
Davis, Walter 152
Dawkins, Johnny 179, 181, *181*
Dayton, University of 86, 90, 97, 125, *126*, 138, 173
Delta State 142
DeNike, Tommy 38
Denver, University of 75
DePaul University *23*, *48*, 48, 49, 51, 52, 53, *57*, 57, 60, 64, 82, 158, *159*, 161, 164
Detroit, University of 129
Dick, John 43, 45
Dillon, John 61
Dischinger, Terry 108, 112
Dittmar, Gus 'Pig' 24
'Dolphins'. *See* Jacksonville, University of
Donnelly, Terry 161
Donovan, Anne 146
'Dons'. *See* San Francisco, University of
Douglas, Sherman 184, 185
Drake, Elmer *85*
Drake University 146
Drexler, Clyde 164
'Ducks'. *See* Oregon, University of
Dukes, Walter *91*, 92
Duke University *2-3*, 87, 90, 112, 116, *117*, 119, 122, 129, 152, 179, 181, 188
Duquesne University 40, 47, 67, 76, 94

Eastern League 18
Edmond, Pete 24
Egan, John *110*, 112
Ellison, Pervis 'Never Nervous' *180*, 181
Englund, Gene 47
Erickson, Keith 119
Ethridge, Kamie 146
Everett High School 156
Ewing, Patrick 164, *166*, *167*, 167, 169, *171*, 172, 173, 174, 176, *177*, 178, 179
'Explorers'. *See* LaSalle University

'Fabulous Five' 70
'Falcons'. *See* Bowling Green University
Farmer, Larry 137
Ferrin, Arnie *55*, 55, 56, 60, 64, 67, *69*
'Final Four' 103, 112, 119, 122, 125, 126, 130, 131, 137, 138, 139, 141, 148, 152, 158, 161, 167, 169, 173, 176, 183, 188
Finch, Larry 137
Fisher, Bob 47
Fisher, Harry 27
Fliegal, Bernie *36*
Florida State 136
Floyd, Eric 'Sleepy' 164, *167*, 169
Ford, Phil 152, *154*
Fordham University 32, 45, 94
Freeman, Coach 'Buck' 30
'Friars'. *See* Providence College
Furman University 90, 92

Gale, Laddie 43
Galiber, Joe *74*
Galileo High School 38
Gard, Eddie *81*, 84
Gardner, Vern *67*, *69*
Garland, Gary 161
Geneva College 17, *17*
Georgetown University *25*, 45, 52, *150*, 164, *166*, *167*, 167, 169, 172, 173, 174, 176, 178, 179, 186
George Washington University 82
Georgia, University of 169
Gerson, Rip 30
Gilliam, Armon 183, 184
Gilmore, Artis 130, *131*, 131, *132*
Givens, Jack 'Goose' 140, *141*, 153
Gminski, Gene 152
Gola, Tom 90, *91*, *92*, 94, 96, *97*, 189
Goodrich, Gail *118*, 119, 120, 148
'Gophers'. *See* Minnesota, University of
Graham, Michael, *167*, 172, 174
Grant, Harvey 188, 189
Green, Sihugo 86, 94
Greenwood, David 152, *155*
Grevey, Kevin 140
Griffith, Darrell *164*, 164
Groat, Dick 86, *87*, 87
Groza, Alex 64, 66, *69*, 70, *70*, 73, 74, 74, 75, *84*, 85
Gulick, Dr. Luther H. *10*, 10, 20

Hagan, Cliff *86*, 86, 94
Hall, Jeff 181
Hall, Joe B. 140
Hamline University 17
Harkness, Jerry 112
Harlem Globetrotters 87, 101, 146
Harp, Dick 100
Harris, Lucy 142
Harvard, University 18, 21
Haskins, Clem 129
Haskins, Don 122, *125*
Haverford College 17
Havlicek, John 105, *105*, *107*, 108, 110
Hayes, Elvin 125, 126, 129, 167
Haywood, Spencer 129
Hazzard, Walt *118*, *119*, 119, 148
Heathcote, Jud 156, *161*, 161
Heaton, Bob 161
Heinsohn, Tom 86, *92*, 94
Heitz, Ken 124
Henderson, R.B. 24
Hetzel, Fred 120
Heyman, Art 112, *117*
Hill, Bobby Joe 122, 124, *124*
Hillhouse, Art *37*, 37
Hiram College 19
Hirsch, Walter 85
Hobson, Howard *43*
Hogan, Frank *81*, 82, 83
Hogue, Paul *108*, 108, *109*, 110
Hollyfield, Larry *135*
Holm, Bob 47
Holman, Nat 30, *31*, 64, *74*, *75*, 75, *76*, 76, 78, *79*, 84
Holy Cross College 18, 64, *66*, 66, *68*, 70, 80, 94
'Hoosiers'. *See* Indiana University of
Houbregs, Bob 90
Houston, University of 125, 126, 152, 164, 167, 169, 170, 172, 173, 174
'Hoyas'. *See* Georgetown University
Hoyt, Richie *107*
Hundley, Rod 86
Hunneke, Harry *34*
Hunter, Les 112

Iba, Hank *49*, 49, 52, *58*, 60, 61, 74
'Illini'. *See* Illinois, University of
Illinois, University of 18, 19, 27, 40, 64, 74, 88, 94, 119, 173
Imhoff, Darrall 103, *104*, 105, 108
Immaculata College *142*, 142
Indiana, University of 18, 47, *88*, 90, *91*, 108, 112, 148, *151*, 152, *152*, *155*, 155, 164, 173, 183, 184, *185*, 185, *187*
Indianapolis Olympians 75, 85
Indiana State *7*, *50*, 154, 155, 156, 158, 161
Intercollegiate Athletic Association 20, 21
International Athletic Association 21
International Training School of the Young Men's Christian Association 10
Iowa, University of 16, 17, 96, 97, *120*
Iowa State 55
Ireland, George 34, 112
'Irish'. *See* Notre Dame University
Irish, Edward S. (Ned,) *33*, 33, 34, 35, 40, 41
Issel, Dan 129, 130
Ivy League 17, 18, 47

Jackson, Michael 172
Jacksonville, University of 130, 131, *132*
Jaracz, Thad *124*
'Jaspers'. *See* Manhattan College
'Jayhawks'. *See* Kansas, University of
Jensen, Harold 178
Johnson, Earvin 'Magic' 7, *113*, 154, 155, 156, *157*, 158, *161*, 161, 186, 189
Johnson, Marques, 139, *139*, 140, 148
Johnson, Steve 164
Jones, K.C. 94, *94*, *95*, *96*, 96, 97
Jones, Wallace 'Wah Wah' 64, 66, *69*, 70, 75
Jordan, Johnny, 34
Jordan, Michael 7, 19, 164, *169*, 169
Journal American 83
Jucker, Ed 108, *109*
Julian, Alvin 'Doggie' 64, *65*

Kaftan, George 64, 66, *68*
Kaighn, Ray 17, *17*
Kallenberg, Dr. Henry F. 17
Kansas, University of 15, *15*, 45, 56, 81, 87, *88*, *90*, 90, 98, *100*, 100, 101, 119, 122, 132, 139, 145, 146, *151*, 179, 185, 186, 188, 189, *189*
Kansas State 86, 186
Kaplowitz, Danny *37*, 42, 43
Kareem Abdul-Jabbar. *See* Alcindor, Lew
Kase, Max 83
Keaney, Frank *32*, 33, 57, *64*
Kearns, Tommy 100
Kellogg, Junius *80*, 82
Kelly, Pam 146
Kelser, Greg 156, 158, 161
Kenon, Larry 137
Kentucky, Univerity of 7, 20, 35, 41, 42, 43, 45, 47, 48, 52, 53, 55, 57, 60, 61, 64, *65*, 66, 67, *69*, 70, 73, *74*, 74, 75, 76, 78, 83, 84, 85, *86*, 86, 87, 88, 90, 92, 94, 96, 97, 98, 99, 100, 101, 103, 105, 108, 110, 116, 119, 121, 122, *124*, 124, 125, 126, 129, 130, 136, 137, 138, 139, 140, 141, 142, 145, 148, 152, 154, 156, 158, 164, 169, 170, 173, 174
Keogan, George 49
Kerr, John 'Red' 88, 94
Kerris, Jack *73*
King, Bernard 152
King, Dolly 42
King, Stacy 188, 189, *189*
Kinsbrunner, Mac 30
Klukofsky, Eli 85
Knight, Bobby *107*, 108, 137, 139, 148, *152*, 152, 155, 164, 183, 184, 185
Kotz, John 47
Kramer, Barry 112, *117*
Kramer, Ken 37
Krivosh, John *34*
Kron, Tommy *124*
Krzyzewski, Mike 181
Kurland, Bob 'Foothills' 48, *49*, 49, 51, 52, 53, 56, 57, *58*, *59*, 60, *61*, 61, 74, 189

Lacey, Edgar 119, 120
'Lady Bruins'. *See* California, University at Los Angeles, (UCLA)
'Lady Statesmen'. *See* Delta State
Lanier, Bob *129*, 129, 130, 131
Lapchick, Joe *56*
LaSalle University 42, 90, 94, 96
'Last Chance Tournament' 121
Lattin, David 122
Lavelli, Tony 75
Layne, Floyd 75, 85
Lear, Hal 97
Lee, Butch 152
Lee, Greg 137, 139
Lee, Keith 176
Leonard, Bob 90, 94
Levingston, Cliff 164
Levy, Seymour *74*
Lewis, Guy 169, 170, *171*
Lieberman, Nancy 145, 146
Line, Jim 85
'Lions'. *See* Columbia University
Littlefield, Clyde 24
Lobello, Cy 42
Loeffler, Ken 94
Long Beach State 132, 146
'Longhorns'. *See* Texas, University of
Long Island, University (LIU) of *37*, 37, 38, *40*, 41, *42*, 42, *43*, 43, 47, 66, *83*, 83, 84, 85
Los Angeles Lakers 102, 122, 161
Los Angeles Sports Arena 126
Louisiana State University (LSU) 90, 92, 129, 158, 164, 179
Louisiana Tech 146
Louisville, University of *97*, 97, 103, 129, 139, 140, *150*, *164*, 164, 167, 169, *171*, *172*, 179, 181, *190*
Lovellette, Clyde 86, 87, 88, *88*, 90
Loyola of Chicago 43, *73*, 74, 75, *84*, 85, *110*, 112, 116, 136
Lucas, Jerry 86, *104*, 105, *106*, *107*, 108, 110
Lucas, John 137
Luisetti, Angelo 'Hank' 37-40, *38*, *39*, *40*, 47, 48
Lynn, Mike 119
Macauley, 'Easy Ed' *71*, *72*, 73, 75
MacGilvray, Ron *90*
McCarter, Andre 139
McCray, Lawrence *133*
McCray, Rodney 164, *165*
McGill, Billy 112
McGill University 10
McGuire, Al *152*, 152
McGuire, Dick 55
McGuire, Frank 99, 100
McKinney, Horace 'Bones' *58*, 61
Macklin, Rudy 164
McLain, Dwayne 178
McLain, Gary 176
Madison Square Garden 32, 33, 34, 35, 37, 40, 41, 45, 53, 55, 56, 60, 61, 64, 75, 78, 81, 82, 85, 86, 88, 142
Mager, Norm *74*, 78, 85
Manhattan College 32, 34, 82, 83
Manning, Danny *174*, *184*, 185, *186*, 186, 188, *189*, 189
Manning, Ed 186
Maravich, 'Pistol Pete' *128*, 129, 145
Maravich, Press 129
Marin, Jack 122, *123*
Marquette University *23*, 139, 148, 152, *152*
Martin, Bill 172
Maryland, University of 94, 137, 146
Mason, Eldon *28*
Massimino, Rollie 176, *179*
May, Don *126*
May, Scott 139, 148, 152
Melchiorre, Gene 'Squeaky' 76, *76*, 78, 85
Memphis State *133*, 137, 176
Mercer 90
Merganthanler, Elmore 56
Merson, Leo 37
Metropolitan Basketball Writers Association 41
Meyer, Ray *48*, 49, 51, 57, 158, 164
Meyers, Anne *145*, 145
Meyers, Dave 137, *138*, 139, 140, 141, 145, 148
Miami, University of 120
Michigan, University of 99, 116, 119, 120, 152
Michigan State 154, 156, 158, *161*, 161
'Mighty Macs'. *See* Immaculata College
Mikan, George *23*, 48, 49, *50*, *51*, 51, 52, 53, 56, *57*, 57, 59, 60, 64, 75, 87, 158, 189
Milcheaux, Larry 164

Milkvy, Bill 92
Miller, Cheryl 146
Miller, Larry 129
'Miners'. *See* Texas Western
Minneapolis Lakers 61
Minneapolis 'Y' 17
Minnesota, University of 18, 19, 154
Minnesota State School of Agriculture 17
Misaka, Wat *55*, 55, 67
Mississippi College 142
Mississippi Valley State 179
Missouri, University of 55
Modzelewski, Stanley 'Stutz' 48, *49*
Moncrief, Sidney *158*, 158
Montana State 27
Montclair State College 145
Moore, Dinty *38*
Morgan, Ralph *18*, 20
Morris, Everett 34
Mount, Rick 125, 129
'Mountaineers'. *See* West Virginia, University of
Muhlenberg 52
Mullin, Chris 176, *176*
Mullins, Jeff 112, 116, *117*
Murphy, Calvin *128*, 129
Murray State 186

Naismith, James 7, *10*, 10-15, *11, 12, 14, 15*, 16, 17, 45, 56, 98, 147, 185
Naismith, Maude *14*
Nash, Cotton *116*, 116
National Basketball Association (NBA) 7, 75, 85, 94, 101, 102, 108, 129, 142, 146, 148, 156, 179, 189
National Collegiate Athletic Association (NCAA) 7, 20, 41, 42, 43, 45, 47, 48, 52, 53, 55, 57, 60, 61, 64, 66, 67, 70, 73, 74, 78, 86, 87, 88, 90, 92, 94, 96, 97, 98, 99, 100, 101, 103, 105, 107, 108, 110, 116, 119, 121, 125, 126, 130, 136, 137, 138, 139, 142, 145, 148, 152, 154, 156, 158, 164, 169, 170, 174, 179, 183, 186, 188, 189
National Invitational Tournament (NIT) 41, 42, 43, 47, 48, 52, 53, 55, 56, 57, 64, 66, 70, 73, 74, 75, 76, 78, 84, 85, 86, 88, 92, 94, 97
Naval Academy *26*, 27, 64, 94, 183
Navy. *See* Naval Academy
Nevada Las Vegas 173, 183, 184
Newberry College 92
Newell, Pete 119
New England League 18
New Jersey Nets 185
Newman, George *37*, 42
New Mexico, University of 129
New Mexico State 56, 131
New Orleans Jazz 142
Newton, Milt 189
New York Herald Tribune 34
New York Jewels *30*, 33
New York Knickerbockers 120, 179
New York Times 13
New York University (NYU) 28, *29*, 32, 34, *35*, 35, 37, 41, 45, 60, 64, *72*, 73, 83, 112, *117*
New York World Telegram 33, 34
New York Yankees 148
Niagra 94, 129
Nicks, Carl 158, *160*
North Carolina, University of 27, 61, 99, *100*, 100, 101, *126*, 129, *152*, 152, 154, 164, 167, *169*, 169, 185
North Carolina State 66, 78, 84, 94, 137, *138*, 138, *154*, 169, 170, *172*
Northwestern University 45
Norton, Ken *80*, 82, 83
Notre Dame University *2-3*, 34, *35*, 35, 49, 130, 132, 136, *137*, 137, 158, 164
Novak, Mike 43
Nowell, Mel 105, *107*, 108

O'Brien, Eddie 87, 90
O'Brien, Johnny *87*, 87, 90
Ohio State 17, *25*, 45, 47, 78, 80, 105, *106, 107*, 107, 108, *108*, 110, 112, 116
Oklahoma, University of 45, 64, *66*, 66, 158, *188*, 188, *189*, 189
Oklahoma A&M 41, 48, *49*, 49, 52, 53, 57, *58*, 60, *60*, 61, 64, 74
O'Koren, Mike 152
Olajuwon, Akeem 7, 164, *169*, 169, *172*, 172, 173, 174, 179
Old Dominion 145, 146, 179
'Orangemen'. *See* Syracuse University
Oregon, University of *43*, 43, 45
Oregon State 27, 112, 137, 164, 167
Original Celtics 30, *31*, 75
Orsten, Artis, 122
Otten, Don *57*, 57

Pacific 125
Palazzi, Togo 94
Patino, Rick *183*, 184
Patterson, Steve *129*, 132, 148
Patton Gym 45
Pauley Pavilion 137, 148
Pearl Harbor 48
Pennefather, Shelly 146, *146*
Penn State 94
Pennsylvania, University of 17, *18*, 18, 20, *27*, 158
Peoria Cats *112*
Perkins, Sam 164, 167, *171*
Peterson, Vadal *55*
Pettit, Bob 86, 90, 94
Phelps, 'Digger', *137*, 137
Philadelphia College of Pharmacy 19
Phillip, Andy *64*, 64
Phillips, Mike 140
'Phillips 66ers' 61
Phillips Petroleum Corporation 61
'Phi Slamma Jamma' 169
Pinckney, Ed 178, *178, 179*, 179
Pine, Ken 47
'Pirates' *See* Seton Hall
Pittsburg, University of 45
Podoloff, Maurice 85
Pollard, LaTuanya 146
Porter, Howard 132
Posnack, Max 30
Pressley, Harold 178
Princeton University 18, *20*, 20, 116, 119, 120
Providence College, 129, 183, 184
Purdue University 18, 108, 112, 116, 125, 129

'Quakers'. *See* Pennsylvania, University of Queens College 142
Quigg, Joe 100, 101

'Ramblers'. *See* Loyola of Chicago
Ramsey, Frank *86*, 86, 94
'Razorbacks'. *See* Arkansas, University of
'Redmen'. *See* St. John's University
Rhode Island State 33, 47, 48, 64
Rice University, 24
Ricketts, Dick 94
Riley, Pat 122, *124*
Rivlin, William 85
Robertson, Oscar 86, *102*, 102, 107, 108, 189
Robey, Rick 140, *141*
Robinson, David *182*, 183, *183*
Rodgers, Guy 86
Rollins, Ken 70
Roman, Ed 75, 76, *82*, 84
Romney, Ott 27
Roosevelt, President Theodore 20, *21*
Rosenblatt, Bill 81
Rosenbluth, Lenny 99, *100*
Roth, Al *74*, 75, *82*, 84, 85
Rothert, Harlow *26*
Rouse, Vic *111*, 112
Rowe, Curtis *130*, 130, 131, 132, 148
Rules of the Game, 1892 10-11

'Runnin Rebels'. *See* Nevada-Las Vegas
Rupp, Adolph 'The Baron' 35, 64, *65*, 66, 67, *69*, 70, 73, 74, *74*, 75, 76, 84, 85, 86, *86*, 92, 94, 122, 124
Rupp Arena 174
'Rupp's Runts', 122
Rush, Cathy *142*, 142
Russell, Bill 86, *93*, 94, *96*, 96, *97*, 97, 98, 99, 101, 136, 189
Russell, Cazzie 116, *116*, 119, 120
Russell, John 'Honey', *45*, *47*, 47, 91
Russo, Marius 37
Rutgers University 28, 146, 152
Ruthenberg, John 47

Sadowski, Ed 47
Sailor, Kenny *52*, 52
St. Bonaventure 112, 129, 130, 131
St. Francis of Loretto 94
St. John's University 28, 30, 32, *34*, 34, 35, *36*, 37, 40, 51, *52*, 52, 53, *56*, 56, 87, 88, *90*, 92, 148, 174, 176
St. Joseph's 103
St. Louis Cardinals 87
St. Louis University 60, *71*, *72*, *73*, 73, 74, 88
Sampson, Ralph 164, *168*, 173
San Francisco, University of 76, *93*, *94*, 96, 97, 99, 119, 136
San Jose State *93*
San Marcos Baptist 24
Schaaf, Joey *27*
Schayes, Dolph 60, 64, *72*, 73
Schlundt, Don *88*, 90, 94
Schnittker, Dick 80
Schuckman, Allie 30
Schwartz, Solly 42, 47
Scott, Charlie *127*
Seattle, University of 87, 90, 101
Seikaly, Rony *184*, 184, 185
Selvy, Frank 86, *90*, 90, 92
Seton Hall, *44*, *47*, 47, 92
Sewitch, Mike 42, 43
Shackelford, Lynn 124, 125
Shank, Teresa 142, *143*, 145
Shapiro, Dave *81*
Sharman, Bill
Shechtman, Ossie 42, 43, 47
Shed, Nevil 122, *124*
Sheffield, Fred 60
Shelton, Em *53*
Sherman, Maude 13
Shingleton, Larry 112
Shue, Gene 94
Siegar, Dave 189
Siegfreid, Larry 105, *107*, 108
Sloan, Norm 137
Smart, Keith 184, 185, *185*
Smith, Charles *174*
Smith, Dean 164
Smith, Gene 172
Smith, Leroy *83*
Smith College 13
Sollazzo, Salvatore *83*, 84, 85
'Sooners'. *See* Oklahoma, University of
Southeastern Conference 74
Southern Methodist University 97, 173
Spanarkel, Jim 152
'Spartans'. *See* Michigan State
Spectrum 152
Spivey, Bill 76, *85*, 85, 86, *86*
Springfield College 10, *11*, 17
Stagg, Amos Alonzo *16*, 16, 17
Stallworth, Dave 116, *117*
Stanford University *26*, 37, *38*, 38, *40*, 40, 48
Stillwell, General 'Vinegar' Joe 18
Stith, Tom 112
Stoefen, Arthur *38*
Stokes, Maurice 94
Streit, Judge Paul S. 85
Superdome, New Orleans *163*, 167, 184
Sutton, Eddie 158
Sweek, Bill 125
'Sycamores'. *See* Indiana State
Syracuse University 139-140, 174, 184, *184*, 185

'Tall Firs' 43, 45
Tannenbaum, Sid 60, 64
'Tarheels'. *See* North Carolina, University of
Tarkanian, Jerry 183
Tatum, Goose 87
Taylor, *107*
Temple University 17, 41, 97
Tennessee, University of 152
'Terrapins'. *See* Maryland, University of
Texas, University of 24, 27, 146
Texas A&M 27
Texas Christian University (TCU) 88
Texas Western *122*, *124*, 124, *125*
Thacker, Tom *108*, 108
'The Baron'. *See* Rupp, Adolph
Thomas, Isiah 164, *167*
Thompson, Billy *180*, 181
Thompson, David *135*, 137, *138*, 138, 139
Thompson, John 164, 169, 172, 173, 174, 176
Thompson, Mychal 154
Thorn, Rod 112
Thurmond, Nate 112, *113*
Tolbert, Ray 164
Toledo, University of 52, 83
Torgoff, Irv *37*, 42, 43
Towe, Monty 137
Trgovich, Pete 139
Trinity College 18
Tripucka, Kelly 164
'Trojans'. *See* California, University of Southern (USC)
Tsioropoulos, Lou 86, 94
Tubbs, Billy *188*, 188
Tucker, Gerry 64, 66
Turner, Howard *38*
Turpin, Mel 172, 173, *175*
Tyra, Charlie 97

United Press International (UPI) 75
United States Military Academy at West Point 18, 27
United States Olympic Basketball Team (1960) *107*
Unruh, Paul 76
Unseld, Wes *128*, 129
Utah, University of 53, *54*, *55*, 56, 60, 64, 67, *69*, 112, 122, 124, 164
Utah State 131
'Utes'. *See* Utah, University of

Vallely, John 130
Valvano, Jim *172*
Vanderbilt University 186
Vandeweghe, Ernie 64
Vassar College 13
Verga, Bob 122, 129
Verwey, Jerry *84*
Villanova University 45, 74, 80, 130, 132, 146, 167, 176, 178, *179*, 179
Vincent, Jay 156, *161*
'Violets'. *See* New York University (NYU)
Virginia, University of 27, 164, 169, 173
Vranes, Danny 164

W2XBS 45
Wade Trophy 146
Wagner, Milt *180*, 181
Wake Forest, 110, 112, 173
Walker, Chet 'The Jet', 112, *112*
Walker, Jim 129
Walker, Mayor James J. 32
Walton, Bill 116, 132, *133*, *134*, *136*, 136, 137,*138*, 138, 139, 141, 148, 189
'Walton Gang', 136, 137, 138, 139
Warner, Ed *74*, 75, *82*, 84, 85
Warren, Mike 124, 125, 126, *126*
'Warriors'. *See* Marquette University

Washington, Kenny 119
Washington, Richard *139*, 139, 140, 141, 148
Washington State University 86, *102*, 102, 103, 103, 107, 108, 189
West, Jerry 47, 90
West Championship 55
West Chester State 142
Western Conference 18, 19
Western Kentucky 48, *106*, 129
Westminster of Pennsylvania *34*, 34, 35
West Texas State 48
West Virginia, University of 48, 57, 67, 102, 103, *104*, 112
White, Byron 'Whizzer' *41*, 41, 85
White, Sherman *83*, 84
Whittenburg, Dereck 170
Wichita State 116, *117*, 120, 164
Wicks, Sidney 130, 131, *131*, *132*, 132, 148
Wicks, Sue 146, *146*
Wiesenhahn, Bob 108
'Wildcats'. *See* Kentucky, University of; *See also* Villanova University
Wilkerson, Bobby 148
Wilkes, Keith 137, 139
Williams, Charles M. 17
Williams, Reggie 172, 174, *176*, 176
Williams College 18
Wilson, Tug *58*
Wingate, David 172, 174
Wintermute, Slim 43

Wirth, Leila *144*
Wisconsin, University of 18, 19, 27, 47
Wittlin, Mike *74*
'Wizard of Westwood'. *See* Wooden, John
WNBC 45
'Wolfpack'. *See* North Carolina State
'Wolverines'. *See* Michigan, University of
Women's Basketball *144*
'Wonder Five, The' 28, 30, 32, 33
Wood, Al 164
Woodard, Lynette 145, 146, *147*
Wooden, John 110, *112*, 116, *116*, 119, 121, 124, 125, *126*, 129, 130, 131, 132, 137, 138, 139, 140, *141*, 141, 145, 148, 181
Woolpert, Phil *94*, 94, 96, 119
World War II 48
Worsley, Willie 122
Worthy, James 164, 169, *170*
Wyoming, University of 52, *53*, 125

Xavier of Ohio 186

Yale University 9, 17, 18, 20, *21*, 75
Yates, Tony 108
Young, Bob 100
Young Men's Christian Association *11*, 13, 14, 15, 16, 20, 21, *28*

Acknowledgments

The author and publisher would like to thank Mike Rose, who designed this book, Elizabeth McCarthy, who prepared the index, Rita Longabucco, who did the picture research, and John Kirk, who edited the text.

The Bettmann Archive: 9, 14(top right), 16, 19(both), 25(top, bottom), 26, 27(top), 28(bottom left), 41(bottom), 43(bottom), 45(right), 144(all three).
Carol Blaze: 145(bottom).
Brompton Picture Library: 37(bottom), 38(top).
Courier-Journal and Louisville Times: 97(bottom).
Malcolm Emmons: 2-3, 6, 108, 110-111(all three), 116(bottom right), 117(all three), 120-121(all three), 123, 124(top), 126(top right), 128(bottom right), 129(both), 130-131(all three), 133(top left), 134, 135(bottom), 136(top), 137, 138-139, 139(right), 140-141(all five), 147, 148-149(both), 150-151(all six), 152(bottom), 153, 154-155(all four), 156-157(all three), 158-159(all three), 160, 164-165(all three), 166-167(all four),168-169(all three), 170-171(all four), 172-173(all four), 174-175(all three), 176-177(all four), 178, 179(top), 180-181(all four), 182-183(all three), 184(bottom), 185, 186-187(all three), 190.
Field Enterprises, Inc/Newspaper Division: 84(top).
Immaculata College: 143, 145(top left).
Immaculata College, photo by Lyn Malone: 142.
Indiana University, Sports News Service: 88(left), 91(bottom).
Library of Congress: 21(bottom).
Naismith Memorial Basketball Hall of Fame, The Edward J. and Gena G. Hickox Library: 10-11(all three), 12(bottom), 13(both), 14(bottom), 15(bottom), 17(both), 18(top), 20, 21(top), 24, 30(both), 32-33(all three), 35(bottom), 37(top), 39, 44, 45(left), 46-47, 48, 49(top), 51, 52(bottom right), 56(top), 61, 64(left), 65(bottom), 66-67(both), 71, 72, 73(bottom), 74-75(all three), 76(bottom), 77, 78, 87(bottom), 88-89, 90(bottom), 92(both), 94-95(both), 100(bottom right), 102-103(all three), 104-105(all three), 107(bottom), 115, 116(top right), 118, 119(bottom), 122, 125(bottom), 126(bottom), 128(bottom left), 145(top right).
New York Public Library Picture Collection: 38(bottom), 52(top right).
Michigan State, Sports Information Office: 161(bottom).
Providence Journal-Bulletin Photo: 49(bottom).
Rutgers State College Office of Sports Media Relations and Information/ Photo by Nick Romanenko: 146(top left).
UPI/Bettmann Newsphotos: 12(top), 14(top left), 23, 25(center), 27(bottom), 28(top right), 29(both), 31, 34, 35(top), 36, 40, 41(top), 42, 50, 53, 54-55(all three), 57(both), 58(bottom), 59, 60, 63, 64(right), 65(top), 68, 69(bottom), 70, 73(top), 76(top), 79, 80-81(all three), 82-83(all four), 84(bottom), 85, 87(top), 90(top), 91(top), 93, 96(both), 97(top), 98-99(all four), 100(top left), 101, 106, 107(top), 109(both), 112-113(all three), 116(left), 119(top), 124(bottom), 125(top), 126(top left), 127, 128(top), 132, 133(top right, bottom), 135(top), 136(bottom), 138(top left, bottom left), 152(top), 161(top), 163, 179(bottom), 184(top).
University of Kansas Sports Information Office: 15(top), 56(bottom), 146(bottom).
University of Kentucky Athletics Association: 69(top), 86.
University of Oklahoma Athletic Department: 52(top left), 58(top), 188-189(all three).
University of Oregon Archives: 43(top).
University of Pennsylvania Sports Information Office: 18(bottom).
Villanova University Sports Information Office: 146(top right).